HOW TO TRANSFORM YOUR LIFE
THROUGH ASTROLOGY

The astrological term for the movement of the planets in the heavens is the *transits*. It is commonly and mistakenly understood that the transits dictate our lives. The function of the slower-moving planets, Saturn, Neptune, Uranus, and Pluto, is to force you through mental, emotional, or physical tensions to make a change in your life. Knowing the forces working on you means you can actively exploit them to reach the destiny you want.

Other Bantam Books by the same author
Ask your bookseller for the titles you have missed

ROBIN MACNAUGHTON'S SUN SIGN PERSONALITY
  GUIDE

HOW TO TRANSFORM YOUR LIFE THROUGH ASTROLOGY

Robin MacNaughton

BANTAM BOOKS
TORONTO · NEW YORK · LONDON · SYDNEY

HOW TO TRANSFORM YOUR LIFE
THROUGH ASTROLOGY
A Bantam Book/May 1983

ISBN 0-553-23203-7

Published simultaneously in the United States and Canada

Bantam Books are published by Bantam Books, Inc. Its trade-
mark, consisting of the words ''Bantam Books'' and the por-
trayal of a rooster, is Registered in U.S. Patent and Trademark
Office and in other countries. Marca Registrada. Bantam
Books, Inc., 666 Fifth Avenue, New York, New York 10103.

PRINTED IN THE UNITED STATES OF AMERICA

O   0 9 8 7 6 5 4 3 2 1

The hero keeps going and even his ruin was only a subterfuge for his achieving final birth.
                                                            —Rilke

Contents

Preface

This book was conceived because so many people over the years have asked me the same question: "Everything in my life is crazy; what's happening in the stars, and when will it all be over?" In this book I attempt to thoughtfully answer that question—perhaps because I want people to finally stop asking it—but also because I have a serious desire to shed some of the light that I have absorbed from all of this "stuff" over the years. Astrology is just stuff. It's a system of thought that carries its own symbology, and it has a very complicated way of ultimately getting down to the same point as other systems—systems as varied as Eastern mysticism and nuclear physics.

Perhaps in a way, it's more interesting because there is such a plenitude of emotional, psychological, and spiritual messages inherent within the symbology. Much of what I will say in this book will be antagonistic to much of prevalent belief, and you may think I am a fool for my heavy emphasis on positive thinking. I am complacent about such antagonisms. There are many people who would prefer to believe in nothing, or in the cruel inevitability of their own death. They would definitely hate this book and wouldn't be the sort of people who would buy it in the first place.

Ideally, I would like to help the reader understand the profundity of the "craziness" and, in the process,

understand something more about himself and perhaps come away looking at his life in a new way. The
purpose of astrology is to use the stars to live beyond
the stars. It can't hurt. It might help. At any rate it will
give you something challenging to think about.

This book has two parts. The first is a guide to
understanding the metaphysics that underlie astrology.
Its purpose is to help each person to understand more
about the dynamics of his or her own life and with that
knowledge have more control over it. Each piece within this section was written as a whole unto itself and
may be read as such, out of sequence.

The second section is a condensed guide to understanding the spiritual meaning inherent within certain
planetary cycles that often instigate personal crisis. By
looking for your sun sign in the tables in the back of
the book, you will be able to pinpoint the time when
specific planetary energies are interacting with your
own nexus of energies. If you also know the sign of
your ascendant, the relevant sections will also be
applicable.

The nature of this book is inspirational. It is guaran-
teed to move you at least a little beyond the tiny circle
of yourself and enable you to enjoy yourself and your
life that much more. It is a book to read and reread in
times of depression, psychological crisis, fear, emptiness,
hopelessness, and any time you feel you need a boost.
If you come to this book in the middle of an emotional
crisis, it will be very difficult for you to close it feeling
sorry for yourself. Instead, you will start to see your life
as an exciting, mysterious adventure, where anything
can happen and each day ushers in a dawn of possibility.

I wrote this book from my heart for those of you who
want to grow through the light of esoteric wisdom.
With it goes my testimony of mystical possibility, since

I have lived that of which I speak. The development of consciousness is the only way to liberation and self-mastery, and only when there is self-mastery is there freedom—freedom from pain, from terminations, and from annihilation. The true sage feels no pain, regardless of his outward situation. Through his persistent striving toward greater meaning, he has come to exceed himself and his life conditions.

This book is a celebration of the transcendence and the human possibility that can be yours. The more the spirit is made conscious, the more the life becomes creative and the greater is the light that radiates from it. It is my serious hope that the contents of this book will bring you further along in the struggle.

I

ASTROLOGY
AND TRANSFORMATION

The Function of Astrology in Our Daily Life

Astrology is significant only because it is a tool for self-knowledge. By understanding the electromagnetic interchanges of the other planets with the earth and with our own unique electricity, we have an opportunity for greater self-realization. The astrological term for the movement of the planets in the heavens is the *transits*. It is commonly and mistakenly understood that the transits dictate our lives. Hence, people are willing to pay money to astrologers to find out their future.

However, although this type of fortune telling *is* done, sometimes accurately, it is also misleading. For, as the late psychiatrist Carl Jung once said, "What happens to a person is *characteristic of him*." And anyone who has developed his will and his higher self is impossible to predict for.

The challenge of man's existence is to direct his own universe. His despair is that he is convinced he cannot. As Kierkegaard so aptly put it, despair is the disrelationship of man's lower self to his higher self and is suffered by the person "unaware of being characterized as spirit." As such it is essentially life *consuming*.

The function of the transits of the slower-moving planets, Saturn, Neptune, Uranus, and Pluto, is to force man through specific mental, emotional, and physical tensions that will cause him to feel, both consciously and unconsciously, the need to create a release, which will often require some sort of action. The more conscious a man is, the more actively he creates his own fate. The mind of a highly developed spiritual being has a more powerful effect than that of any transiting planet. As the late mathematician P. D. Ouspensky once said, "The microscopic living cell is more powerful than a volcano—the idea is more powerful than the geological cataclysm." However, most people utilize very little of the potential power of their minds and prefer to assign power to forces outside themselves.

The struggle toward greater consciousness is always a painful one in which man fights himself at the same time that he drives himself in the desire to be ultimately free. Thus, the path of the spiritual seeker and the analysand, committed to moving beyond themselves, takes the predictable curve into the dimmest reaches of the self. As in the journey through Dante's *Inferno*, the experiences along the way may be both frightening and momentarily deadening. Nevertheless, they must be experienced fully if they are to be passed through to greater light and greater freedom.

In alchemy this state of consciousness is known as *Nigredo*. It is the stage in which the base lead of the spirit dissolves into blackness, which must occur before it can transmute into the brilliance of gold, the everlasting supremacy of the higher self: fully conscious man freed from personal fear; a creature who is master of his inner world. However, the price of such divine peace is the sacrifice of his innocence, his ignorance, and his illusions.

Our illusions are both costly and comfortable, in that they create a panoply of "certainties" that anesthetize us from our fear of the unknown. The function of the slow-moving planets is to stimulate life situations that challenge these "certainties," opening the psyche to an intuitive awareness that the unknown is not nothingness. It is merely meaningless—until we make the choice to create our unique meaning.

Because these planetary cycles are usually associated with personal crises, the transits of Saturn, Neptune, Uranus, and Pluto are commonly feared and associated with pain. They are, however, potentially, rich growth-producing periods. During these times, whatever disintegrates in one's life—marriage, job, intense love affair—is no longer enriching the spirit and is separating it from a harmonious union with the personality. Once again, to quote Kierkegaard, "a young girl is in despair over love and so she despairs over her lover because he died or because he was unfaithful to her. This is not a declared despair. No, she is in despair over herself. This self of hers, which, if it had become 'his' beloved, she would have been rid of in the most blissful way . . . this self is now a torment to her when it has to be a self without him."

Man's most profound pain arises not from his losses but from the rigidity of his attachments. When there is no attachment, there is no pain. That is not to say that we should not feel deeply or develop attachments. On the contrary, we should allow ourselves to feel so deeply that we move beyond all strictures of feeling, to a purer, unconditional quality of love that is not tainted by pain. The pain of jealousy has far less to do with the degree of love than with the rigidity of fear. And possessiveness has to do with the insecurity of ownership, not with the heartfelt response to the inner beauty of another human being.

With the development of a higher consciousness, all strictures begin to dissolve until the self experiences, in the words of St. Paul, "Nothing moves me, yet everything moves me." In the meantime each experience of pain is an opportunity to *work* beyond pain. But man must decide in each crisis whether he is going to *work* and what he is going to *make happen*. To borrow a line from the *I Ching*, "Now he sobs, now he sings." But before one breaks out into the joyousness of song, one must be willing to empty oneself of one's tears.

Fate Versus Free Will

The ability to predict an individual's future through astrology is based on a sophisticated knowledge of symbology and logical propability, and the possession of psychic ability. To put it simply, if two planets come together in a certain angular relationship, given the interference of a complex of other existent planetary factors, one might say that it is probable that a certain influence will be felt. However, one cannot say for sure, *from the horoscope alone*, on what level—mental, emotional, or material—this influence will be felt, or if it will *necessarily* be felt at all. The mysterious element that upsets the entire system is the power, degree of consciousness, and level of awareness of the individual mind.

Because the horoscope represents our *potentiality* as well as our present proclivities, it is impossible to tell from studying that alone whether the person represented by that horoscope has actually grown to actualize that potential, or is operating on a more mechanical level of his energies. Experience usually leads one to assume that in most cases very little of the person's will is being used. Indeed, most people come to astrologers, not to gain greater emotional insight and self-awareness, but simply because they want to be told what to do. Essentially, they create a psychological transference with both the astrologer and the subject. It is a moment of regression, in which the "child" wants to be assured by the "parent" that everything is going to be all right, without having to do anything himself to make it all right.

There is nothing wrong with this *if* it is regarded as only a first step to a deeper and greater awareness. However, as with all transferences, this one carries its own power, and it is a power that begins to take over and to have a life of its own that is usually devoid of any validity. The result is that, instead of using the symbology of astrology as a tool for a greater awareness, the individual personalizes it and diminishes his or her own powers to it with the attitude that the planets dictate the life, instead of the character of the person. Not only is this attitude ignorant, it is self-destructive and not conducive to growth or personal responsibility.

Astrology is merely a symbology. It is not a final answer to anything. Its potential importance is that it can help us learn about ourselves and others through a kind of numerical metaphor. All the answers we need are already within us. The problem is that most people are not even conscious enough to pose the right questions.

Advanced mystics know that nothing is more powerful than human consciousness *at its potential.* However, most peoples' minds run on a relatively low wattage. They are moved along by their own routines and exist in utter subjectivity—*contained within* the tediousness of their own lives.

The tenor of an average human life is to be pulled toward death by the dynamic forces of the outside. The electromagnetic force fields of the planets act as programming devices on the brain. The results are mental and emotional tensions and fears that must be released through some sort of expression or activity. However, that outer event is really being generated from the unconscious mind. Life is actually a Rorschach of individual subjectiveness. But when the consciousness changes and expands, the life changes and expands, and the quality of personal events change.

We are not pawns in an arbitrary universe, our life determined by external mysteries. We are our own power, however strong or weak that power may be. To be happy, serene, and free, it is necessary to develop that power. And along with it comes a greater sense of possibility.

In the following pages I hope to provoke new perspectives that may lead to that sense of greater possibility. At the very least, I hope that the material will provide some thoughtful moments that may help a hopeless person begin to question his or her own pain.

Introduction to the Slow-Moving Planets

The planets Saturn, Neptune, Uranus, and Pluto have the slowest rates of motion of all of the planets in the zodiac. Because of this, they remain in one sign or constellation longer (usually for one to several years), and their vibrational influence is experienced more intensely. These planets are also the farthest away from the earth and therefore have more of a "cosmic" import on human existence as opposed to the sun, moon, Mercury, Venus, Mars, and Jupiter, which carry lighter vibrations and are associated more with routine, mundane matters.

Actually, Jupiter, the planet of expansion, forms a sort of metaphysical bridge between the "inner" and "outer" planets and can be associated with a cycle of spiritual or creative expansion. However, this depends on the individual level of evolution. In a less-evolved individual, the experience of Jupiterian expansion can be in the area of appetite and indulgence rather than spiritual growth.

As the slow-moving planets make their imposing vibrations felt in daily life, our challenge is to achieve a more conscious awareness. Their profound impact on our lives (as opposed to the other planets) forces us into situations where we often feel at war with ourselves. Their force, like a torrential rainstorm, is impersonal, yet commanding. Therefore, the individual who is rigidly defined by a routinized existence and who has very little inner nurturance will be thrown off balance more by this force, which appears to be circumstance.

The unconscious person is inevitably a victim of "circumstance," because he is at the mercy of the forces of his own depths. The vibrations of the slow-moving planets "irritate" the depths of the unconscious until the drives group into clusters of compulsions, sometimes filtering through conscious thought patterns and always seeming to manifest themselves from the "outside."

However, the ancient Hermetic axiom "as above, so below" shows that there is no differentiation between heaven and the human mind, or hell and the human mind. One doesn't have to travel anywhere. One has only to be. But first one must choose how he wants to be, and just to be able to make that choice takes an above average level of awareness.

Most people are dissatisfied, joyless individuals seeking to escape either their inner turbulence or their emptiness, and the motivation for their search is their desire to annihilate what they don't want to look at. The cycles of experience fostered by the slow-moving planets force man to go inside himself to see what's there and to confront his fear that what he wants may never be. During one of these cycles the individual often finds his way into therapy because nothing "out there" is enough. Nothing is fulfilling enough to eradicate the deep pain in his soul.

This is an important and necessary first step. For only in knowing one's deepest reaches can one come to accept them and monitor them and, in the self-knowing, accepting, and monitoring, become one's only control. One individual cannot change the world or force another person to fall in love, but when one's self-awareness and self-love are well-developed, one will naturally attract positive, loving experiences. To get there, one must develop every aspect of the self, the mind, the body, and the spirit. Each individual must constantly strive toward his potential, in order to achieve greater realization of his life. The often painful cycles initiated by the energies of the slow-moving planets are ripe periods for working toward a greater becoming.

The pain that is often experienced in these periods, as life situations break up, is the pain that comes from being forced to look into the self, and seeing or feeling not enough is there. Such a crisis arouses feelings of inadequacy, created by a self that is fragmented and not self-trusting. Often, when the breakup of a relationship is very painful, the degree of pain experienced is equal to the degree of unexpressed rage or to the fear of ultimate aloneness. The self does not trust that it can have an affirmative, loving experience that will be defined by a generative feeling of inner joy. Because it cannot give real love to itself, it can do no more than demand love from another. And this love assumes an awesome importance because it is the love and acceptance that the self needs and cannot generate for itself.

When one really knows oneself and is constantly developing oneself and comes to love and accept oneself, one becomes the power of love, and there really can be no loss. At this point the consciousness is totally objective, free from defenses, excuses, fantasies, illusions, and fears. The consciousness is not absorbed with grasping for love. Instead, it expresses love freely and becomes a positive vehicle that is at once generative and magnetic.

This point in evolution is a challenge to move toward. The crises created by the slow-moving planets bring that challenge into focus. In the midst of such a crisis it is important to ask yourself, what is it that I now must learn to have a richer, happier existence? What is it that is lacking in myself? How can I better myself to deal with life more painlessly? How can I better myself to deal with this situation less painfully? What am I really afraid of? To get what I want most? What do I have to do? What should be my first step? How, in the long run, could I be better because of this experience?

It is important that you believe that all of these questions can be answered and accomplished. The ultimate positive experience that results from actualizing these answers is, in fact, the individual's destiny, which is his challenge to claim. The crisis cycles of the slow-moving planets give us the opportunity to choose our preferred direction, and any soul who chooses against his own growth is one who chooses a lifelong marriage to suffering.

The Human Need to Transform

A human being's greatest misfortune is not his experience of pain but his resignation to it and his unwillingness to move beyond it. At the same time, the only remedy a person has for his or her own pain and terror of aloneness is a total willingness to grow. Implicit in this growth is a psychological, spiritual transformation that brings the mind to a state of being that is ultimately positive, light, and free. The more infinite a human being grows, the more his or her life becomes like a fascinating, ceaselessly changing adventure. However, the more the mind clings to limitation, the more it will be dominated by the essential emptiness of existence.

Life crises are psychological rites of passage in which consciousness has the potential of growing, expanding, and freeing itself. As the energies of the slow-moving planets catalyze crises, we are given the opportunity to grow, transform, and transcend our patterns of suffering. Without these experiences, life would be like a television test pattern, and we would be hopelessly enmeshed in a mechanical existence, where all movement would be exterior to the sense of being. As a result of such rites of passage, our previous attachments change in importance and our personal requirements are no longer the same. By passing through painful experiences, a person has the chance to be freed by them and from a cluster of fears that were once controlling. To look back

14

from this place of new self-trust is to see a lonely dog howling at the moon and to shudder. At the same time there is the security that one will never go back there, that life will never again be quite so terrifying.

Yet this assurance is only possible when the mind has made a commitment to itself to grow beyond itself emotionally. The fact is that most people stay in the same emotional place and re-tread their own pain. They are unaware that another quality of being is possible. Their lack of awareness is so deadening that they cannot even begin the pilgrimage toward something greater.

For the average human being, the life experiences catalyzed by the major planetary cycles include emotional suffering. But these cycles are necessary for the awakening of the higher, wiser, inner being, which is the only portal to lasting freedom from pain. Potentially, these planetary cycles can bring a greater meaning to living. The essence of this meaning is greater strength, awareness, peace, joy, and trust in one's unique higher nature. This higher nature encompasses each person's emotional, intellectual, and psychological potential. But it can only be achieved through a deep inner desire that becomes a drive toward greater wisdom, joy, and meaning. In the following pages, I will attempt to make the ups and downs of this journey more immediate. The rest is up to the individual.

The Experience of Transformation

The purpose of life is more life, and eventually that life can become the light of consciousness. That experience is the potential of the challenge that the energies of the slow-moving planets bring to our existence.

Every individual today is faced with the same existential dilemma of seeking and finding an affirmative meaning to his life that will provide him inner sustenance. At the same time, this quest is the source of profound anxiety that is rooted in a creaturely fear of loneliness, isolation, and alienation.

Most people project this anxiety onto a love situation. This works for a while, as long as either the content or the discontent, as the case may be, supersedes the individual's confrontation of his own existential dilemma—his ultimate aloneness and his ultimate death. However, each person must ultimately return to his or her self, if only through death or the death of the loved one.

When a deep, intrinsic meaning to life is unfolded from the inner reaches of consciousness, not only is the anxiety of life alleviated, but the terror of death is overcome. For this quality of well-being, romantic love is not enough. For romantic love, by its very nature, implies attachment and thereby reinforces the individual's creaturely vulnerability to the person to whom he or she is attached. If an ultimate meaning is attached to a person outside the self, then the conditions of meaning are both limited and circumscribed by the conditions of that outside person's existence and not by the individual's will. Love has its own life-affirming meaning. However, the degree to which a person attempts to tie his sense of emotional and psychological possibility to that experience alone, is the degree to which he will be limiting himself from an exciting, liberating self-exploration.

It takes courage to break out of a rut and search for something more. It also takes courage to look directly at the unacceptable contents of one's inner reaches. And it takes the most courage to actively attempt to transform the darkened experience of selfhood.

Transformation does not happen organically, apart from will. Most people leave this earth much the same or even worse than the way they came into it, and that is a tragedy for an existence so capable of greater life.

The philosopher Spinoza attested that those who strive long enough eventually become the power of the striving. It is through this power alone that transformation is possible and the anxiety of life and death alleviated by a rich inner trust of a continual becoming. However, even with striving, transformation takes time. There are no shortcuts to ridding oneself of the human to evolve into the superhuman. On the contrary, there are constant obstacles that can bring about an endless number of regressive periods where the brain seems to be stretching toward heaven but the feet are still dangling in hell. Even when the individual has intuitively tuned in to the transcendental, he will still be dragged down day after day by the demands of the material. This must be lived through and balanced with the inner, spiritual world.

It is important to live life to its fullest, to grow and ripen. Astrology is an important tool because it can make clear the symbolic, soul meaning of various periods, cycles, and experiences of life. Through this prism, what had formerly appeared to be a painful, personal disaster, annihilating to the very essence, can be seen from a more detached and expansive perspective as an opportunity to become more aware, to make positive, life-affirming changes, and to grow, thereby into a wiser, happier person.

That does not mean that the pain evaporates—and it shouldn't. Emotional pain can produce a great deal of growth, for it goads us into making frightening changes that we might otherwise avoid. It also heightens our sense of compassion for others. It holds the possibility that, with enough striving and experience, we ultimately can come to a point of serene dispassion.

The pain that accompanies the transformative process is caused by one's resistance to surrendering the defensive, fearful part of oneself. However, as transformation unfolds, and the human changes into the superhuman, the mind rides on each moment with a higher, intuitive awareness, flowing with time, balancing the inner with the outer, the lower with the higher. While living life, loving, and making the necessary choices, the evolving human trusts, despite material demands and disappointments, that time is the herald of infinite possibility and that life is really the unfolding of a higher, purer, vastly creative power that exists in limitless quantities within the self.

At each step of the spiritual journey, one should question and evaluate the meaning and validity of each experience. Question the books. Question the teachers. Question your feelings as well as any lack of feeling. But do allow the answers to take you somewhere, if only to further questions. The deadly moment comes when the dynamic stops and the pulse fades. Many inquisitive people begin and end here. But for those who "know" that there must be something more and yearn to find it—the seekers of an experience that defines life itself—the teachers will come, the answers will come, and the light will come with the seeking. If you are among this group, trust this and never stop trying. One day, you will wear your new self like a new skin, and your heart, your mind, your very life force itself, will glow with the promise of More.

The Experience of Saturn: Is That All There Is?

The electromagnetic effects of a transit from Saturn result in mental dullness, emotional weariness, and a profound feeling of discontent with the inherent emptiness of life's structures. Life, work, love, close relationships, often become less satisfying and, at moments, seem entirely stripped of meaning. The lesson of this is that the area of life that exudes this dullness is spiritually meaningless and in need of a generative sort of nourishment. This is a time when one is more consciously fearful, when a free-floating anxiety permeates the psychic atmosphere. Living becomes a bleak, even onerous experience to the degree that the individual is dependent and defined by his external structures. At the same time, an area of the psyche unconsciously seeks greater freedom, and one is convinced that a vacation from the job, partner, the appearance of a new love, will offer the much needed release.

However, the degree to which the person yearns for a vital change seems, quite often, to be the degree to which he stagnates out of fear. In mythology Saturn murdered the children of his brother Uranus and fed them to him. This is symbolic of the destructive potential of fear and how it can brutally destroy our creative sense of freedom (symbolized by Uranus). In the Tarot the card of the devil is ruled by the planet Saturn. The devil is represented as a horned beast, which reflects the ancient Greek satyr Pan. Hoofed and horned, he symbolizes the bondage to the lower, animal level of the human being who does not attempt to transcend himself. Saturn's rulership of this card is typified by the constricted almost backward development of the person who, out of fear and inertia, does not attempt to move beyond what appears to be limitation.

The transit of Saturn is a time when one may feel overly insecure or overly pressured by the on-the-job performance, anxious about the attentions of one's partner, deeply anguished at the thought of possible abandonment or betrayal, lonely for love, fearful that it will never materialize. On the deepest levels of the psyche, the needs and fears are resisted, and this creates in the outward personality a strong degree of tension that often manifests as anxiety, depression, or, when the defenses are particularly intricate, apathy.

The person who is largely unconscious will not be aware of the sources and tides of discontent. His most likely choice of behavior will be to create some sort of escape to ease the heartache. Drugs, alcohol, taking to one's bed through illness—any of these outlets may be attempted to alleviate the tension that has become physical. Yet, when each experience wears off, the entire being becomes compressed in the vice of a unique personal vision of emptiness.

Saturn forces the individual to see the essential emptiness of life. Try as he may, life is not the way he would like it to be ideally, and his inner vision is assailed with the meaninglessness of so many of life's structures. Saturn represents the cold, gray dawn of consciousness. It is the vision of the flawed love, the experience of the encroachment of the burdens of the material world, the feeling of bondage and boredom in the routine of a love relationship. This is the time when one feels emotionally and sexually cold, controlled by the sense of obligation to personal and professional responsibilities, and dulled by the emptiness of one's own life.

By consciously confronting these feelings one has an excellent opportunity to establish greater meaning and greater awareness for oneself. The challenge of this period is to trust the emptiness and to begin a search for experiences that have richer, more profoundly sustaining meanings. It is necessary now to build and create from the sense of nothingness, to establish new life structures that free the self from the feeling of being controlled by "fate," fear, or anxiety.

That could perhaps begin with the search for a new job, project, career, course of study. Perhaps it could also involve the forming of new relationships or the restructuring and regenerating of old ones. On the other hand, maybe what is needed is a separation from one's partner in order to discover that one can also stand alone. Saturn challenges all of our dependencies by making us suffer because of them. When the individual has learned his lesson, he comes away with the awareness that he has a responsibility to himself to make the right choices, and when he makes the wrong choices or, worse, no choices at all, he has a responsibility to himself to learn from that experience and to grow past it. The nature of Saturn is material. Therefore, it has to do with action, with trial and error. Its electromagnetic effect on the brain is that it challenges us to strain for new possibilities by making us feel frustrated, confined, or disgusted with the status quo.

The ancient, ignorant, astrologers were of the opinion that one should just go to sleep under the effects of this transit and advised people that there was no point in doing anything because it would only end in disappointment and frustration. On the contrary, the lesson of Saturn is precisely the opposite of passivity. Its message is *do*! If you are unhappy with your life, do something about it. If you are unhappy with yourself, do something about it. And if your choices do not work out, try, try, and try until something does. The mistakes we make in life are not only important but necessary. They are our opportunities to move beyond ourselves to experience a greater aspect of ourself.

However, the very first step in the journey is that you must ask yourself why you are unhappy. The answers you get back may be multifarious—meaningless work, unsatisfactory love life, disappointing sex life, embarrassing weight problem, boring friends, not enough security to look into the mirror and smile. However, regardless of the number or the kind of responses on your particular list, there is really only one answer: You are not happy with yourself. You. In the flesh. All alone. Against the world. And the worst part is that you don't know how to be.

The most important thing to realize from this conclusion is that this is really okay, for just to have this conscious awareness is the first step in what could become an exciting journey through yourself. In addition, keep in mind that there is no guru, saint, or wise and gifted psychiatrist who was born with conscious answers either. Yet everyone was born with the liberating spark that remains unconscious until we work to unfold it. Saturn is the planet of work. Work on every level. At its most significant it represents the work we must do on the material level to transcend the material and ourselves, our limitations and our pain.

Saturn's importance as a transit is that it gives us an opportunity to take some baby steps toward something greater. In doing so we are forced to question meanings.

The result of which is that we see that there are no external structures that can alleviate the anxiety of death. Potentially, this questioning will bring the awareness that there is nothing outside the self, including one's greatest achievements, that can meaningfully substitute for the liberating experience of the higher, mystical self. This understanding begins with self-acknowledgment, self-awareness, self-acceptance, and self-love, and extends to a transpersonal love of the beauty of others and of their potential inner reaches, and love of the beauty of love as it exists in all aspects of the world. One of the results of the mystical experience is the feeling of an intense, unbearable love for life and all the beauty that life has to offer, which includes the potential beauty of humanity. When this experience is reached, after years of study and disciplined meditation or contemplation, the individual personality, with all its problems and fears, dissolves into a beatific experience of love that is so powerful that nothing in life can approach the intensity of such pure bliss.

This is the potential of humanity at its peak. No other ego-bound satisfaction can approach this. If this were not true, there would be no suffering artists, no suicidal movie idols, and no multimillionaire magnates mortified by their own aging and quivering in anxiety at the prospect of their own death.

To quote the late psychiatrist, Carl Jung:

> The inner man continues to raise his claim and this can be satisfied by no outward possession. And the less the voice is heard in the chase after brilliant things of this world, the more the inner man becomes the source of inexplicable misfortune and uncomprehensible unhappiness in the midst of living conditions whose outcome was expected to be entirely different. The externalization of life turns to incurable suffering.

Even self-love is not enough to obliterate the despair intrinsic to man's mortality. That takes yet another step—one that most human beings never even approach in a lifetime. The ultimate meaning is to be found, not in self-awareness, but in *total* awareness. The influence of Saturn provides the first stirrings in that direction.

This truth is verified in the mysteries of alchemy. The alchemist's endeavor to change lead into gold is a symbolic one that many foolish, greedy chemists mistook at the time. The success of this venture is the creation of the philosopher's stone, which is not a hunk of metal, but a state of purified consciousness. It was claimed in the traditional writings that any man who had achieved this painful, dangerous undertaking was capable of all things and had the magical power to control the world from without. For the philosopher's stone was considered the "father of all miracles," including healing and immortality, and such it is, symbolically.

However, its secret is that it is spirit and not matter. The golden philosopher's stone is the soul, the expanded consciousness of the alchemist who is beyond mortality in that he "knows" that physical death is not a termination of experience but a translation of experience.

In alchemy Saturn is associated with the base lead that is to go through the arduous transmutation to gold—divine, mystical awareness. Lead is the darkness of the unconscious being. The opportunity of the pain that the transit of Saturn provides is our potential for refusing to accept the pain or to grow old defined by it. But first we have to control our fears so that ultimately we can move beyond them. Secondly, we have to struggle to convince ourselves that we do deserve more. Thirdly, we must make choices and take affirmative action to enrich and affirm the self, not escape from it. Fourthly, we must, through therapy and disciplined mystical study, be willing to risk the unknown and relinquish the limitations that are comfortable and secure. Finally, we must never, never give up trying. For Saturn is the ancient taskmaster, out to see that anyone who doesn't really try will fail. The human self will not exceed himself who does not assiduously assert himself. The path to mystical enlightenment, away from the darkness of existential meaninglessness, is the one requiring constant vigilance and ceaseless effort. The final result is a being beyond choice, defined by a consciousness radiant with possibility balanced around a radiant inner center, and serenely secure in the power of its SELF and of the eternity of its life.

The Experience of Uranus:
Why Is All This Happening to Me?

The life lesson that transiting Uranus catalyzes into our experience is the challenge of finding the most constructive use of freedom in order to become a more complete individual. Uranus is also associated with loss and points a cosmic finger at what we must lose or give up in order to free ourselves of our limitations.

The experience of Uranus is often a difficult and painful one, because it always appears to come about unexpectedly. As such, it is considered by many astrologers to be the cosmic bolt from the blue. Uranus's force is as sudden and as disruptive as an earthquake. And it can elicit the same psychological effect, especially if one is particularly concerned with security.

The negative emotions associated with Uranus are helplessness and abrupt loss. Often one feels like one has been punched in the solar plexus for no reason. There is an overwhelming feeling that one is being victimized by an irrational, meaningless stroke of fate. The kinds of experiences involved are usually a sudden breakup of a marriage or love affair, a freak accident, the instantaneous death of a loved one, and perhaps the loss of a job.

While, subjectively, all of these experiences can be intensely painful, looked at from a larger, objective perspective, they are not meaningless absurd turns of events. Each has a reason, each is an opportunity for becoming something more, and each is potentially a gateway to a greater awareness.

Uranus is the planet associated with the unpredictable. Many astrologers feel that it is impossible to really determine how its transit will affect a life. However, it is my opinion that this can be surmised to a reasonable extent by delving into the psyche and determining the degree to which the person is repressed, the degree to which they are being controlled by their own dependencies and fears, and by what area or areas of life are most profoundly affected by these dependencies and fears.

Under the influence of a transiting Uranus it is likely that the person who is very rigid and fearful will be hit hardest in an area in which he feels most vulnerable. However, any loss that comes into their life through the abrupt change will involve something or someone they no longer really need but nonetheless are still clinging to.

Uranus annihilates our false supports and makes us suffer because of our dependencies. It demands that we stand on our own two feet or at least appreciate the necessity of trying to. As such, it inspires a more individualistic attitude toward life. Uranus is the great awakener of consciousness. Its energies open up the drowsing mind and inspire it to suddenly grasp intuitive truths. Potentially, it can bring a new sense of reality. However, it demands personal change and that the individual becomes more objective, and more aware. In the end, it demands that he transcend the personal to embrace a more expansive awareness, that he move beyond the confines of his little box of living or suffering to view himself more dispassionately and others with greater compassion.

The conditions that come to an end under this planet are the conditions that the soul no longer needs for growth. Usually they are conditions that are holding the personality back from becoming more. The personality has become so secure in the externals that it has taken to sitting on itself, contented to watch the world pass by. The transit of Uranus will not necessarily change a person and his attitudes. But it will very likely change the conditions surrounding him and give him opportunity for serious thought and constructive action.

The relationships that break up under the influence of Uranus are stagnant, "secure" shelters that have become comfortable, empty retreats. They are no longer generative, rich with mutual growth and mature loving, but have become, instead, bastions of need. Uranus reminds us that there is no security outside of the self. Each person we love is but a resting place to learn and grow through the experience of loving. When that growth stops, there is no further cosmic purpose to the union. Time moves on and so must our life and our souls.

On the other hand, those individuals who have been working hard to grow emotionally and spiritually may experience this transit in a totally different way. Suddenly, a new condition exists in the life that was never there before, and doors are open, beckoning the way to new possibilities. This new condition could be a new love, a new marriage, a newborn child, or perhaps an exciting new personal challenge. Uranus is also the planet associated with a high octave energy of excitement. Anything can happen under its influence. It just depends on where we let our minds take us.

Many astrologers believe that a relationship born under a "bad" aspect of Uranus (square—90-degrees or opposition—180-degrees) has little chance of lasting. This is not necessarily true, although it appears that it is often the case. Again, the duration of the relationship is based less on the nature of the aspect and more on the degree of maturity, awareness, and self-knowledge that is characteristic of the person at the time. If the individual is in his or her early twenties, then it is more likely that this is a love at first sight situation that will lose its emotional glamour with time. However, if the person is older, a great deal wiser, and a lot more experienced, this could be the stimulating new connection that the soul needs to become something more.

On its highest level, Uranus is associated with genius, the kind of knowledge or understanding that comes intuitively. If the mind and spirit are highly developed, this transit could be experienced, not as an external event, but as a higher octave thought process that awakens the entire being and, through this awakening, eventually changes the quality of existence.

Whatever the ultimate outcome of the transit, the energies of Uranus are high voltage vibrations to the psyche, instigating change and forcing spaces and channels for greater growth and richer experiences. Potentially, it can ignite exciting new moments in life and make the individual aware of the constructive possibilities of freedom. However, before that is possible, the individual has to get beyond his own constricting fears in order to envision his life as an open-ended passage of time, ripe with the richness of potentiality and limited only by his own neurotic fears, defenses, and unwillingness to grow.

As Dane Rudyar, the brilliant, renowned astrologer put it, "The essential characteristic of man is that consciously and deliberately he may always become greater." This is each person's birthright—if he attempts to claim it. The function of Uranus is to demolish the life preserver to allow us to experience swimming alone and actually liking it.

The Experience of Neptune:
I Know There Must Be Something More

Because Neptune is a much slower moving planet than Saturn or Uranus, its effect by transit is more subtle and less dramatic. Due to the nebulous nature of its vibrations, its experience may be more on the level of consciousness than on the plane of events. Also, if there is a strong natal relationship between Neptune and the Sun, this influence will be felt more profoundly.

In general, the nature of this planet is oceanic. Neptune was the Roman god of the sea, and he ruled over its fathomless mystery, its coldness, loneliness, and timelessness.

Neptune, like the sea, has a dissolving power. At the same time, it can be an instrument of unification, like the sea washing over the land. Neptune's essence is fluid, undefinable, and watery, and water is associated in astrology with the emotions. When its vibrations affect an individual by a close transit to his sun sign, a subtle or even unsubtle sense of confusion, unrealized longing, and need for something *more* will permeate his consciousness and control his sense of well-being. This can be experienced as a vague, passive discontent or as an active seeking of the fantastic, not only to escape, but to dissolve into ecstasy. Drugs, alcohol, erotic love—all the classic elements of the ancient Greek Bacchanalia—usually come into play on this level. Rapid fluctuations of feeling are taking place now. One day the discontent is solved by an inspired solution, only to be followed three days later by apathy and confusion. One week one revels in the glamour of a new, grand love, only to experience not much later, a sense of evaporated illusion.

Neptune is the power of illusion. It is also the need for it. We all have, at one time or another, wanted to be captivated by another person's glamour and reduced to passivity, made helpless by our own desire. Often under the "spell" of Neptune we feel this helplessness. We want to become more through an experience that's so much larger than life that it takes us out of our sense of everyday living. At the same time, under Neptune's influence, a sense of confusion distorts our mastery of the issue. We long for the bliss of "paradise" and, at the same time, are painfully aware of the tedious impingement of the mundane world. Not only are the mind and the emotions confused, but the will is also weakened. We wait for an answer from the outside, and until it magically arrives, this can be a time of floating from wistfulness to fantasy and coming to no constructive conclusions.

The emotions are at their peak now, and because of this, the sense of discontent can not only dissolve a marriage but also create a situation of unrequited love. When you don't know what you want except what you don't want, you have no control over the direction of your life because you are not employing your will.

The longing for love experienced under the transit of Neptune has less to do with individual loneliness than with a need for the oceanic experience of "falling" in love. It is a desire to be lost in and controlled by a sea of feeling, to be made emotionally embryonic, nurtured, comforted, and sustained. It is the yearning to be assured that one will not have to grow old alone, for the future lies like a black, horizonless sea for the individual who has quietly despaired of the reassurance of such a lasting union.

However, the impersonal cruelty of Neptune, like the cold destructiveness of the raging ocean, points out the illusions in such an attitude through the experience of disillusionment. Part of its message is that we are all alone, regardless of the illusion of appearances. However, because this awareness is too unbearable to be consciously confronted without mystical insight, this is a time when the average individual is tempted to seek oblivion in other ways, usually liquor, drugs, or sex. That, of course, is not to say that everyone who experiences the transit of Neptune will become a drug addict or an alcoholic. Yet this denial of the mundane world—where one does not have to think, fear, or experience anxiety— is the nature of the Neptunian influence on its lowest levels.

On the higher levels, Neptune is associated with all forms of creativity and especially those of music and film. It generates the suspension of disbelief required for a creative act, the alpha consciousness that channels subconscious material through conscious awareness and merges the two into an inspired outpouring of thought. On this level, which is no longer passive, the "something more" is created by the individual will. The result being that, after and because of the process, the individual himself has become something more. The negativity of discontent has sparked the positiveness and possibility of creation. Through this experience, the individual is no longer measurable but has been transformed into an instrument of possibility and through action has become possibility.

On the highest level, Neptune is the planet associated with mysticism. Here the profound discontent has to do with the finiteness of everyday human experience.

What is sought now is the beatitude of transcendence, and what the individual wills is to be beyond the everyday self. It is at this stage of consciousness that the second part of the Neptunian truth becomes operative. That is—yes, man, as an individual is alone, but as a being he is not separate. He is a vital part of a greater, vast, glorious whole and as such is, *at his potential*, the glory of life itself in all of its affirmative aspects. At his highest, an individual is grace and he is eternity and he is all of the beauty that the earth has to offer. This mystical awareness comes when the lower ego dissolves into the higher self or spirit. The yearning for completion is satisfied and the love urge changes from the personal eros to the transpersonal agape, love of the potential of all things, love of the potential of life.

Neptune breathes of a paradise of being. It makes us yearn and search, and learn clarity from the illusions that we uncover through our experiences. Through this essential elevation, it offers us the potential of moving beyond *maya*, the mental world of illusion, of being more conscious, and ultimately of becoming super-conscious. Its vibrations separate man from superman defined not only by a state of awareness but also by a nonegoistic sense of compassion.

Neptune is a difficult planet because its vibrations are completely incongruent with the demands of the material world. It puts us in the mood to escape, write poetry, be mystics, or fall madly in love. Therefore, it can wreak chaos with the working logic of one's mentality.

Neptune's transformative strong point is its creative potential. As a life stage, its shadowy discontent nudges us to create more from life. To do this, we must make a conscious effort to direct our will toward a greater awareness, so that each day, each month, and each year heralds the promise of More.

The Experience of Pluto:
Who Am I Really?

Pluto is the planet of transformation. As such, it rules over Scorpio, the sign of death, regeneration, and the divine mysteries. Pluto is the slowest-moving planet in the zodiac, remaining in one sign or constellation for many years. Likewise, its effect upon the consciousness is also slow, subtle, profound, and sometimes barely perceptible, depending on the level of awareness of the individual.

Pluto's energy is mysterious, yet its power is profound. Astrologers associate its discovery, in 1930, with the creation of the atomic bomb. From ancient mythology to today, it has been associated with all aspects of the underworld, including the Mafia, and it figures prominently in the horoscopes of great mystics and spiritual figures, as well as in the charts of some of the most ruthless, power-hungry political dictators.

These facts are of importance only in that they illustrate that on a metaphorical level this planet has to do with the mystery of power. At the highest level of consciousness Pluto symbolizes the purified being who, time and again, has been through the cauldron of experience, each time becoming more self-aware, always seeking a greater degree of enlightenment in a perpetual struggle toward total illumination.

At its lowest expression it represents the demonic power of the unconscious unleashed in compulsions, obsessions, or the ruthless, manipulative drive for material power.

In its transit, Pluto acts as the cosmic eliminator, dredging up the unconscious dross that our defenses find almost unbearable to deal with. It can bring on severe mood swings and identity crises, obsessive-compulsive love affairs, painful abandonment situations, and in extreme cases even death itself. Understandably, all of these experiences sound rather horrible. However, what I want to strongly stress is that what actually occurs during the course of a Pluto transit depends on the level of the individual's consciousness and the content of his unconscious. The person who is deeply repressed, unaware, and indifferent to growing will experience a much greater degree of stress than someone operating from a higher fluid level of consciousness. With a higher quality of mind, the Pluto transit can be experienced on a more positive level as the gradual emergence of a new identity, the conception of a new creative project that is transformative, the development of a new, more positive life-style, the discovery of a new philosophy or form of therapy that is generative, or the attainment of a higher step on the spiritual path itself, characterized by a more profound and pervasive intuitive awareness.

The very potential of the Plutonian experience is a heightened consciousness, which, when expanded to the highest spiritual levels, can bring about a degree of transcendence that annihilates even the fear of death itself. However, to get there, one must grow through many mental and emotional changes until finally, the limited ego is exceeded by the total experience of the higher self.

In order to do this, one must live with a higher, positive force in mind, work seriously at knowing the self through psychotherapy and ceaselessly try to eliminate the self-destructive tendencies that are retarding self-love. It is also important, as a psychological process, that one become aware of his own particular demons, those unacceptable impulses that are shameful or guilt producing, detach from their affect, and integrate them into the personality in a balanced, conscious way so that they cease to be a controlling force.

The lessons of Pluto are the hardest because they always seem to be the most emotionally obfuscating. Essentially, they point to the message that a human being must always become more to alleviate his own suffering. First, one must know oneself and one's underworld, and then one must internalize the discipline of Saturn, learn the dispassion and higher understanding exemplified by Uranus, and experience the compassion and love of Neptune. When one has reached that point, one will have transcended many of his human limitations.

The journey is a lonely one, fraught with self-destructive fears and doubts, moments of exhilaration and periods of severe existential alienation. And always, the demons that pull one backward are the dross of one's unconscious that has yet to be integrated.

Pluto is the planet of extreme force and profound change. However, the outward changes of Pluto differ markedly from the abrupt changes of Uranus because they always spring from a condition that has been festering under the surface for a very long time. The relationship that ends under Pluto is the one that both people have known for years is hopelessly in trouble yet have clung to compulsively. Its pain swells in their depths and its pressure strains outward, yet they continue miserably to renew the bonds out of an obsessive terror of aloneness.

Quite often intrinsic to the Plutonian situation on its most painful levels—both by transit and when Pluto is prominently placed in the natal chart—is the feeling of being engulfed by one's own irrational sense of dread and fear, to the extent that one's sense of possibility is markedly diminished. Another way the influence of this planet appears to exert a stranglehold is through obsessive-compulsive behavior, the most common of which is usually the "passionate" love affair that carries as its underlying price a sacrifice of the self, which often results in severe disappointment and self-hatred. There *is* a demonic aspect to eros. In the emotionally repressed individual, the Plutonian force is demonic in that it consumes the conscious personality. At an advanced stage, there is no identity except in relation to the force itself and the love object, and this is the key to the obsession. When this driving force is annihilated through the termination of the relationship, the identity is also annihilated, and one is left with a death-in-life situation that represents the power of Pluto at its most profoundly destructive.

Pluto is the planet of both death (emotional or physical) and life (regeneration and renewal). On either level its power is both profound and awesome. The overwhelming attention paid to the recent murder trial of Jean Harris—a dignified, upper-class, middle-aged woman who murdered her lover of many years over the presence of a younger woman—was because it was something many people were sympathetic with as it brought to light their own potential darkness. This awareness of the unacceptable contents of the inner depths, although not an easy experience, is necessary if these feelings are to be integrated into the conscious personality. It is only when such urges remain unconscious or suppressed that Pluto wields such a demonic power.

The Plutonian vibration is potentially most destructive for the individual who has a poor sense of self and no rich inner life. Such an individual can easily be taken over and enslaved not only by their own unconscious impulses but by the unconscious demonic impulses of everyone else as well. Ultimately, the only salvation for a person of this type, who might seem fated for a life of intense emotional pain, is to regenerate his entire sense of self by developing a stronger, brighter core and a self-sustaining sense of creativity. Over time, if he works at it, his life will change and become more vital as the quality of his choices changes, and slowly, his decisions will come to be determined by an affirmative sense of freedom rather than by the former neurotic needs, dependencies, and compulsions.

This is the generative aspect of the Plutonian force. Its challenge is to accomplish this sort of psychological resurrection which is usually brought about by an intense emotional crisis. A dam breaks. The strain of self-resistance becomes too strong. At long last, there no longer is any person, relationship, fantasy, under which to hide, and the result is devastating. However, Pluto's lesson is that this is what must be destroyed—these old, repetitive, self-annihilating patterns. Pluto announces that there is a total person under all the dependencies, obsessions, compulsions, and escapes, and in a cold, impersonal manner, Pluto commands it to come out and try to stand up, or suffer the real pain of death—suicide. Even if this sort of obsessive person does not, out of the depths of mortal agony, make an actual suicide attempt, nonetheless, the repetitive pattern of such self-destructive choices is ontologically suicidal, in that he or she is losing the life to pain.

Many people enter psychotherapy for the first time under an intense Pluto transit because the pain of an unaffirmed self has become unendurable. A positive confrontation of this pain opens the way to further self-knowledge, self-affirmation, and release from bondage.

What one eventually learns from the entire deathlike experience of the crisis is that once one finally lets go of the old destructive forms of behavior and learns to trust the higher aspects of the self, one's life will begin to renew itself because it begins to mirror this affirmative consciousness. Potentially, Pluto can show us that love is never lost but is assimilated into our consciousness and built upon. A person who has loved many times knows this from experience, while the individual who is afraid both to trust himself or to trust someone else doubts it and builds his life around this doubt.

Pluto represents the possible renewal and regeneration of every aspect of life. Its mystery is hinted at in mythology by the lesser-known fact, that Pluto, the god of the dead, was also known as the god of wealth, who ruled over the precious metals hidden in the earth. This is a metaphor for the precious jewels of wisdom lurking in the dark depths of the unconscious mind. Although Pluto was known as an unpitying god, he was by no means evil. After he kidnapped Persephone, the goddess of spring, and brought her to the underworld to be his bride—only to eventually release her for six months of the year—he solemnly entreated her to think kindly of him, telling her that she was the wife of the "one who was great among the immortals."

Pluto's potential is immortality. Its limitation is death. Its mystery is that it is both. Pluto's marriage to the goddess of spring symbolizes that intrinsic to the death-like situation is the potential of rebirth.

This concept of the marriage of death and renewal is seen in many of the mythologies: the Hindu god Shiva is the god of destruction and also of life, the Egyptian god Osiris was murdered by his brother Set, only to rise to new life twenty-eight days later, Christ was crucified and subsequently resurrected. The trial of Christ can be seen as an allegory of the spiritual ascent of man: his suffering, as the suffering of the man who is not spiritually enlightened; the sacrifice implied in the crucifixion, as the sacrifice of the layers of human consciousness that separate us from the divine spark; and the nimbus that surrounds his head after the crucifixion, as the inner light that is experienced when one has achieved cosmic consciousness.

The message behind the death-and-rebirth myths is that, potentially, we are our own saviors, to the degree that we are willing to change.

The challenge now is to look to the highest aspects of the self, to affirm the wisdom, the capacity for joy and love, and then to transcend the lower negative ego self through becoming a state of higher being. Essentially, it is to turn oneself inside out, from heart to mind to soul, until the entire being is a brighter color. This is a very long, slow process, fueled by effort, experience, and a relentless will. Each painful emotional-spiritual trial along the way is a step toward becomes, the greater is the soul's power to sustain one in moments of crisis. An individual who attempts to transcend his crises through an assertive search for a greater meaning is one who will expand throughout his life rather than diminish with the encroachment of age.

What Pluto symbolizes in totality is the potential struggle and journey from man to God, or the highest light of mind. It is the darkened consciousness of man taking a trip, not so much through life, as through the mind in time. The very voyage itself, toward the release of the mind's trapped light, is a lonely, frightening one, as Dante evokes in his *Inferno*. Most people are not aware enough to even consider making it. So they live out their lives like stagnant pools, only dimly reflecting the light of the sun.

Pluto initiates that turning point in consciousness wherein everything that had previously been meaningful dies off, making way for the beginning of a higher stage of growth. As the individual's life-props dissolve before his very eyes, he enters the fathoms of the abyss. It is a state between worlds—an engulfing, deadening sense of nothingness, devoid of even the light of a sustaining vision. This most painful of all Plutonian crises is the profound, almost suicidal, despair that annihilates the very foundation of an existence. This particular experience, which is termed by mystics as the dark night of the soul, is also referred to as the opening of the third eye. In alchemy, it is the stage of *Nigredo*—the breakdown of the lead (of consciousness) into utter blackness before the emergence of the radiant stage of gold, or the sun of the higher being.

But Pluto is also the doorway to the beatific experience of oneself. The price that it extracts for passing through the portal is total surrender of the will to the existence of the higher force within the self. However, the important point to understand is that intrinsic to the dying or surrender of the old self is its own rebirth. But just like an infant, the higher self is born only through labor. After the individual has suffered his own particular period of labor and self-confrontation, at the wondrous moment of release and self-transcendence, he "knows" intuitively that he is his own mother, father, lover, friend, and god, and that from now on the aloneness of life will never again be loneliness, because he knows he exists as an intrinsic part of something larger, and vastly meaningful.

As radiant and as ecstatic as this moment is, it is just the beginning. It is a point of awareness in a newborn consciousness that must grow and continue to expand through time. Pluto engenders a consciousness of becoming in which the opposites of the self, the good and the bad, the heights and the depths, the beauty and the ugliness, are all united in a greater sense of joy, serenity, and a more profound experience of self-acceptance that becomes self-sustaining. The mind is no longer at war with itself. Out of the darkness of consciousness, a tiny, brilliant center has arisen. At first, it is frail and minuscule. At times it is dimmed by the intensity of unbalanced emotions. However, with relentless commitment to the striving towards one's own higher state of being, the center grows larger and brighter, until eventually its light fills the person up like an inner radiance, which actually begins to show in the face. That "light" is so life-sustaining and enriching that all crises cease to be formidable when the personality chooses to live consciously through it.

Regardless of the diminishing quality of external circumstance, the bad moments are only moments in the larger passage of time, while the good moments somehow give the assurance of more. There is an awareness, regardless of one's age, that time, far from being a herald of obsolescence, is instead the harbinger of more. With this attitude, death itself is to be regarded as possibility. Among the great mystics, death bears the same enthusiasm as a wedding in our culture. It is an initiation of consciousness that is potentially the most affirmative of experiences when one is no longer heavy with the burden of fear.

The essence of the Plutonian journey is infinitude. This infinitude is the potential of the transformative process, the awakening of the mechanical part of oneself to a higher, brighter, happier being. To arrive there is to arise each day ripe with an inner plenitude and then to look at the sun and to feel that it is inside of you. The good moments are greater, the bad moments have a greater sense of possibility.

When you reach this point, the entire tenor of life changes because your mind has married the radiant power of your being and diminishment is no longer a deathlike threat. Freed from anxiety and fear, you feel more alive and come to say *yes* to life even at is most difficult. Life has become the joy of creation, expressed in every affirmative act. Each day heralds more luminous possibility, and despite everyday dissappointments, the deep inner positivity richens and the mind's light grows steadily brighter to increasingly light the way.

Love and the Slow-Moving Planets

Love is the law of the universe, the great, vast, mysterious feeling that begins with one's feelings for another and extends to the love of oneself through creation and the experience of what is mystically referred to as God.

Through the experience of romantic love or Eros, we have the opportunity to experience a vaster, spiritual love that is the divine breath of life. The force of the slow-moving planets—Saturn, Neptune, Uranus, and Pluto—remind us of the sacrifice inherent in Eros, and often, through the transformation brought about by a particular love experience, they provide us with the opportunity to become more.

Love is the most profound mystery that a human being can ever experience. It's what separates the human from the animal and gives us the potential to transcend ourselves. The reason why being in love has such a positive or even salubrious effect on our sense of well-being is that we feel like we are more than what we are ordinarily. When we love, we feel our unique essence, and through that experience, become elevated above mere existence.

One of the secrets about love is that, that something-more was always inside us just as the enchanted prince in fairy tales was always a prince even when he was cast into the guise of a frog. But through the love of the princess he was transformed into the best of what he was all along. Likewise, through the loving interchange with another person, we grow to become a greater aspect of ourselves and, in doing so, move that much closer to actualizing our potential. Love's importance is that it brings us back to ourselves in the most positive way, and offers us the further possibility of moving beyond ourselves.

The planets Saturn, Uranus, Neptune, and Pluto can be seen as processes of consciousness that enable an individual to unfold into something greater. Each mode of energy typified by these planets affords an archetype of a growth experience in the area of love. Saturn represents our ego-defenses, the controls that prevent us from showing and perhaps acting from our higher love impulses. On its negative level, Saturn is the restrictive voice of pride. It is the anxiety in the face of a condemning other, even if the other is not in fact condemning. Saturn is the anguish of vulnerability, which is in fact the condition of having assigned to another person the power to diminish you. It is the cloying power of shyness and self-deprecation, and it is the proclivity to diminish another out of a need for self-defense.

It might be said that humanly destructive acts are motivated more frequently from fear than violence. Saturn is that fear. It is the capacity to bear a grudge and the desire to get another person first. It is sarcasm and an annihilating sort of coldness that leaves no room for heartfelt communication.

People who have strong Saturn afflictions in their horoscope, Saturn on the ascendant, or the moon in Capricorn usually have profound problems in expressing love. Quite often these people are accused of being cold or unfeeling. In point of fact, their feelings are consciously suppressed as a bone-deep defense against vulnerability. In order to experience love successfully these defenses have to be broken down and transformed through the skill of a very wise psychotherapist. If this is not done, their ego-defenses will determine the quality of their relationships, and diminish their capacity of self-expansion through love. Saturnian people are quite often highly controlling business executives who are successful in the boardroom but failures in the bedroom, where they substitute performance for affection and never know the difference.

When an individual has transcended the Saturnian tendency to erect alienating controls, he is capable of experiencing love. And the moment that the love experience has begun, he has entered into the realm of Neptune. Although Venus is commonly considered to be the planet of love, in reality Neptune is the experience of love on all levels. Venus is what we value in the love object and the kinds of qualities that initially attract us.

Neptune is the phantasmagoria of first love and the flights of fancy and fantasy that accompany all states of being in love. It's what makes love blind, grand, evanescent, and, even when unrequited, glamorous. Inherent to the nature of Neptune is sacrifice. When we fall in love, we sacrifice our self-awareness to the idea of the other person, just as we sacrifice our self-consciousness to the heightened consciousness of the experience. However, at a certain point the narcotic effect has to wear off, and we get ourselves back. When that happens, very often it's like emerging from a dream.

Frequently these experiences become disillusioning— the splendor fades as does the basis for the original spark. Looking back on the experience of a broken love affair and seeing lucidly the multiplicity of reasons for the break, one often wonders how one lost possession of one's senses or tolerated the bad times. The effect of Neptune is that we do lose our normal sense discrimination and for a time take on an extra-sense perspective that has nothing to do with the real world. This perspective is so emotionally powerful that we terminate ourselves in it.

Neptune is the planet of romance. It is also the intangible, mysterious power of Eros that romantic experiences have over the rational mind. Yet, as Rollo May points out in his book, *Love and Will*, "Eros is the power which drives men toward God." Through the experience of Eros it is possible to experience higher kinds of love because the nature of Eros is such that it always "drives us to transcend ourselves."

At the highest level Neptune represents a pure soul love. It is the power of soulful transcendence and the essence of a transcendental consciousness. It is also that longing for more that can never be fully satisfied in an earthly experience. Neptune gives birth to the vague longings that move humanity toward God by instilling profound, unfathomable yearnings in the heart. It is the fullest capacity for loving which transcends the needy ego-centered experience and all limiting ego-defenses. Anyone who has achieved this state called cosmic consciousness has felt dissolved by a radiance that elevates his inner reaches and unites his center with the most positive aspects of nature. The sense of individuality has transcended into a state of universal consciousness, and a feeling of unity. This state is not sustainable, just as all Neptunian experiences are not sustainable. However, it is maintainable through meditation just as the experience of romantic love can be kept alive in the mind through fantasy.

People who have Neptune strongly placed in their horoscope are idealists who have problems maintaining ongoing relationships. What these people are seeking is the ideal love, and the problem is that they are too emotionally confused to even formulate a realistic ideal. Because of this, they often succumb to a glamourized aspect of a person that is salient and superficially attractive. However, when the surface entertainment starts to wane and less attractive personality factors emerge, the Neptunian either feels disillusioned and disinterested or deluded and victimized. The conclusion that these people draw from their lopsided perceptions is that all love is ultimately disappointing and that ideal love does not exist. In part, they are correct. For if you base what you call love on surface entertainment rather than on respect and appreciation of another person's totality, intrinsically this situation will be unsustainable. However, to claim that ideal love does not exist is ridiculous. Ideal love does exist, and each individual has the potential to experience it. However, in order to attain that love, one must first be whole and not emotionally fragmented. Our experiences of falling in love are growth opportunities in which we have the potential of moving toward that whole.

The ideal love is one where two people have grown to such a high degree of completeness that they come to each other as generative wholes rather than as empty containers. Their highest attributes spark the best in each other, so that the relationship catalyzes a higher quality of life for both. With time, the vitality of the union increases because each individual continues to grow and increase. Each year can be measured by the positive changes that enriched each person as well as the overall quality of the relationship. In this ideal love, there is no end to the personal, emotional, psychological, spiritual, and human accomplishments that can be engendered, regardless of age. From this union, both people generate a sense of possibility that comes to define life itself.

The psychoanalyst June Singer terms this whole, individuated personality an "androgyne," meaning that the male and female (animus, anima; active, passive) aspects of consciousness are both equally developed. The ultimate effect of this parity is a personality that is more nearly a totality, and who therefore brings something vital to a relationship, rather than getting lost in it. She goes on to say that relationships between such highly transformed people are most exciting and electric, producing "unbounded energy which can be turned inward and upward, or fed out in a controlled streaming."

Such people drive themselves to dance to life and in the dancing become the dance. They learn from the blending of joys and sorrows, beginnings and endings that the experience of each person is but a long or short parking place, and this need not be sorrowful if one becomes an endless road.

These people begin life with defenses that have to be shed eventually, and through growth, crisis, manage to lose this defensive part of themselves. Trying very hard, despite circumstance and obstacle, straining and struggling for more meaning, they ultimately grow toward that which they want their life to become. With that becoming, they transform themselves into self-realized beings of greater human possibility, which is symbolized by the planet Uranus.

The Uranian vibration at its most constructive epitomizes the ancient Greek spirit *Agape*, love through the spirit for the spirit of another. Uranus rules the sign Aquarius and when the Aquarian Age is referred to, the major reference is to an evolving, less egoistic type of consciousness that is capable of a higher, purer kind of love that emanates from spirit rather than ego-oriented personality.

Uranus is freedom in the sense of autonomy. It is the lesson that we can only love freely and purely when we have first come to know, love, and trust ourselves. The truly free individual, as opposed to the one who remains unattached out of fear of intimacy, is the person who knows that he or she has the resources and the inner power to create from life despite disappointing adversities. At its highest, Uranus leads us to the awareness that all the personal power that we need is already inside us. We just have to learn how to free our minds and let it flow forth.

Uranus is the higher octave energy of Mercury. It is brilliance, genius, electricity, originality, freedom, and innovation. Uranus demands that we shed our psychological fetters to develop into self-realized beings and approach the possibility of a purer kind of love that is free of possessiveness, and fear. It demands that we care from the richness of our centers and that we grow from the quality of that caring. As Erich Fromm put it so beautifully,

> Love is possible only if two persons communicate with each other from the center of their existence, hence if each one of them *experiences* himself, from the center of his existence. Only in this "central experience" is human reality, only here is aliveness, only here is the basis for love. Love experienced thus, is a constant challenge, it is not a resting place but a moving, growing, working together; even whether there is harmony or conflict, joy or sadness, is secondary to the fundamental fact that two people experience themselves from the essence of their existence, that they are one with each other by being one with themselves rather than by fleeing from themselves.

He also makes the crucial distinction between falling in love and standing in it. This is the message that Uranus holds for us.

By transit Uranus breaks up "secure" life situations and challenges us to grow, to become more, and to create more from what we have become. Its message is that each individual should stand, not lean, in love. A loving interchange is abused when it is reduced to infantile gratification, sexual satisfaction, or a cozy security blanket. Fromm points out that this way of using it, "as a haven from aloneness is a normal form of the disintegration of love in modern western society."

Love and sex have become commodities, and human beings have been reduced by their own predatory natures to the kind of abusing based on using. It is an age of voracious libidos and alienated hearts advertised by the question: "What am I going to get?" There are few who are so highly developed, so radiant with a generative self-love that the first impulse is simply to offer some of it.

The Uranian society or Aquarian Age would be a utopia based on the love ideal and composed of highly developed, individuated people who stream forth with a nonegoistic quality of caring. When Uranus is prominently figured in the horoscope, there is, in general, a personal rather than emotional response to situations that is often humanistic in nature. However, when this planet makes hard angular aspects to the sun, moon, ascendant, or Venus, the high octave energy adds a profound current of restlessness to the personality, and the individual is caught in an emotional struggle between the need for love and the need for freedom. Freedom and the use of freedom become a major life and love issue that must be worked at to be resolved. Out of deep-seated fears of feeling engulfed and psychologically smothered, these people sometimes run from the responsibility involved in a love commitment. Often their behavior is emotionally ambivalent and schizoid, what they say they feel bears little resemblance to their behavior, and they seem to be moving in opposite directions simultaneously. They often respond to emotional demands by distancing themselves, and when the threat to their freedom becomes too awesome, they may disappear altogether or instantaneously fall out of love.

Confinement, to the Uranian mind, is like dying a slow death by deep breathing through a wet blanket. These are people who need lots of space, who thrive on change, and who need to feel in close association with another person, a certain degree of mental excitement or else a sickening sense of suffocation will settle in. On an unconscious level, they connect commitment with stagnancy, and when they sense the first signs of a sedentary situation, their hearts cool and their spirits strain to be free. Many Uranian people exacerbate their own claustrophobic anxieties to such an extent that they either avoid relationships altogether through promiscuity or by claiming that there is no one they can find to love. They can also be known to form terrified, uncommitted connections that they are capable of breaking without a backward glance. Sometimes they even develop obsessive attachments to people who are in some way unavailable or equally problematic.

Needless to say, it is not easy to be in love with a Uranian personality type or, for that matter, with anyone who has one or more of the modern planets prominently configurated in his or her horoscope. That is because the vibrations of these planets are of such a high octave that they are impersonal by nature. They have to do with the evolution of mass consciousness, not personal gratification. Therefore, the birth imprint on the personality—whether or not this person cares one way or the other about spiritual evolvement—will have the effect of making the psyche more detached and distant than a personality where these planets are not prominently configurated.

The planets Uranus, Neptune, and Pluto are always prominently configurated in the horoscopes of great mystical and religious leaders, musicians, artists, filmmakers, and the most enduring figures in literature. The goals and gratifications of these people are transpersonal by nature. Currents flow through them that come to define them. Whether or not constructive, disciplined action is taken to direct and utilize these energies successfully, the impulses, often enigmatic in nature, continue to make their claim.

The writer Flaubert is an excellent example of the extreme of this tendency to have a compromised attention span. Compulsively at work on *Madame Bovary*, which took him five painstaking years to complete, he secluded himself in the country and kept his "love affair" with his girl friend, Louise, at the level of correspondence. Finally, when he felt sufficiently menaced by her plethora of letters requesting some proximity, he wrote to her saying, "Louise, let us love each other in art, as the mystics love each other in God."

Saturn forms the bridge between the inner and outer planets, and it carries with it the lesson of responsibility. To love fully is to care responsibly. But that does not mean that one takes responsibility for all of the emotional expectations of the other person. For the other person must also take responsibility for himself, and part of that is to realize the limitations of a love situation and to see the limitations for what they are, divorced from fantasy or wishful thinking. With experience one learns that the facts of a relationship usually don't change. What changes is the individual's willingness to see them clearly.

Uranian, Neptunian, and Plutonian personalities are trying to live and love in a personal world with influences in their psychological makeup that are completely impersonal. Needless to say, they are not people to cling to, and that is the message of these planets. We should not come to the love partner because we need a pillow. We should come because we want to *create* out of what is the best of ourselves the richest quality of an interchange.

Uranian people seek interchanges rather than cozy love nests. Their approach to the world and their relationships is mental and evaluative rather than emotional and possessive. It is meaning that these people are seeking, and because they instinctively comprehend the nature of change, they are forever reevaluating their positions.

When Pluto is prominently configured in the horoscope, especially if it is positioned on the ascendant, there is a similar outward detachment in the personality. However, on the inside these people are extremely complex. They have deep emotional natures and usually a lot of fluctuating moods. Plutonian people are instinctively manipulative and often because of this make life far more complicated than it need be.

The Plutonian personality has a laser beam sort of insight into the machinery of another person's mind. But at the same time, this person holds himself aloof and reveals little or nothing of his own inner world.

Control is the primary motivation, and on a very profound level this need is psychologically tied to the concept of survival. The Plutonian is fiercely independent and has a bone-deep horror of needing anyone outside of himself, because he has an unconscious and sometimes conscious terror of both abandonment and engulfment.

This personality sees life as a battleground where potential loss is played against the promise of gain. To lose is to suffer silently and severely through pride. To win is to gain power.

Power is a focal point in the Plutonian existence. This planet is usually prominent in the horoscopes of political dictators, as well as in the horoscopes of great spiritual figures, who have transmuted its powerful energies to the transpersonal. Plutonian people have tremendous personal power and self-control and an extraordinary sense of concentration. They are capable of great self-mastery, yet in love, their emotions become the battleground of their soul.

These people seek a deep soul-union, and at the same time they have a deep-seated terror of surrendering themselves. Therefore, during the course of an emotional involvement, they are both controlled and controlling. Because they tend toward such extremes and exhibit an all-or-nothing attitude toward life, Plutonians have a difficult time, not only in falling in love, but in finding a suitable partner. These are intensely private, somewhat suspicious people who are not comfortable with instant intimacy. They prefer an intense tête-à-tête with a close, trusted person to chatting with a person with whom they have no rapport.

The vast majority of minds are neither deep nor intense enough for the Plutonian to feel intrigued. And should they find someone who does satisfy these criterion enough to move them beyond their own detachment, their first impulse will be to set up barriers to alleviate their anxiety of either potential engulfment or loss. When, despite himself, a Plutonian falls in love but does not trust the other person, his behavior will be cool, enigmatic, manipulative, and distancing. As time passes the distrust will turn into torments of silent obsession, the manipulations will accelerate, and in the compulsive attempt to gain control of the situation, he will, in fact be losing control of himself. Should a Plutonian be hurt, it is to the very depths. Subsequently they have a very difficult time, both consciously and unconsciously, trusting again. The Plutonian personality never forgets, and once their control panel is reestablished, it is usually with even more buttons. At the same time they maintain a stiff, fiercely independent facade and convince themselves, and everyone else, that they are happier alone. Plutonian people tend to be loners. They are most comfortable coming and going their own way, have very few close friends, and require regular doses of solitude. In relationships, trust and loyalty are essential to their sense of well-being, and when there is evidence that this is being abused, they are capable of cutting a person out of their life without a backward glance.

Plutonian personalities are the most complicated and very often are enigmas to themselves. This is because the archetypical nature of the planet is profoundly complex and esoteric. Pluto represents the mystery of power, the mystery of love and sex, and the mystery of death. And it intricately weaves all of these areas together in the mystery that it holds about life.

Pluto rules Scorpio, the natural eighth house sign, which has to do with sex, death, and regeneration. The significance of these three areas being grouped under one classification is that they are inextricably tied together. Through sexual love we have the possibility of surrendering our ego consciousness in the expression and exchange of an emotional love that is revitalizing and transformative. A French term for the orgasm, is *la petite morte*, the little death. In loving another person, we surrender our self-consciousness to the consciousnes of the experience. Essentially, a part of us dies and is reborn through it, even if that experience does not ultimately conform to our romantic expectations. Analogously, in loving God mystically, we surrender our ego consciousness to the experience of cosmic consciousness.

Through both of these experiences, we are dealing with the potentiality of ourselves. The point is to reach beyond ourselves to become more than ourselves. That is why love is never lost. The specific experience changes, just as our individual consciousness changes. Yet, even if the relationship terminates and we are terribly hurt for a time, we are not terminated. We are something more, whether or not the rigid structure of our ego-defenses allow us to see it. Love is transformative power at its essence. Its very experience is an equation with possibility. What Pluto symbolizes is the profundity of that power.

The Plutonian mystery of sexual loving is self- or soul-affirmation. However, I am talking about the most complete, affirmative sexual interchange, not hit-and-run promiscuity, pornography, or orgies. The latter are transitory entertainment, arising from a sense of self-alienation that is the opposite of self-affirmation. Such activities reflect a profound anxiety about not being able to connect, not only with another person, but more important, with emotional aspects of the self. Fromm trenchantly points out that the orgiastic solution becomes a desperate attempt to escape an anxiety about feeling separate, but that this attempt never creates a real sense of union between two people.

Because loving on the run does not involve care, respect, or responsibility, it cannot lead to an ultimate affirmation of the self. On the contrary, it is a frantic attempt to lose the self in a momentary oblivion, not unlike that of drugs or alcohol in point of purpose.

The degree to which we invest ourselves in an experience of loving is the degree to which we can potentially grow from that experience. However, that potentiality is diminished by the ego's tendency to restrict the experience to a perspective of gain or loss.

Quite often, transiting Pluto triggers love crises. Next to death itself, the loss of love is probably the most profound human crisis. Yet, at the same time, the life-death crisis of love offers a tremendous opportunity for growth if the individual can bring himself or herself to the challenge of seeing his or her life in a larger perspective. Such a crisis is a highly energized time, when the conditions that have broken up have the potential of being rebuilt into something more meaningful and fructifying. It is a time when the person has an opportunity to transcend himself or herself by rising to transcend the limitations of the condition. With the transformation of the crisis, comes the transformation of the individual.

At its highest, Pluto symbolizes the power of the higher self to rise above all human limitations. It is the divine monad or spark of God that is inside every human being. In order for that spark to grow, we must grow on all levels of our being. Essential to that growth is the capacity of keeping the heart open to all of the beauty that exists in life. The heart is the divine center. To the degree that a person has closed it off, he or she has limited his or her capacity to grow and multiply through love.

The energies of the slow-moving planets provide this impetus by electrifying the contents of the unconscious, thereby bringing new forces into the life that have to be dealt with and moved beyond. In the end, there are only two choices in life—stasis or striving. The power of striving is the power of endless possibility. One has only to experience the power and glory of the pathway, to affirm, despite all momentary obstacles, that there really is no other way.

II

PLANETARY CYCLES AND
PERSONAL TRANSFORMATION

Look in the back of the book where the cycles of the slow-moving planets are specifically delineated by date. See where your sun sign fits in and when these planets' energies were or will be relevant to you. Then flip to the appropriate chapters to read about the larger meaning and challenge of these periods and how to become a more creative person through them. Keep in mind that the transit of a planet through a sign goes from 0 to 29 degrees of longitude. The closer it comes to the degree of your individual sun sign, the more intensely its influence will be felt. In addition, these planets go through two to three phases of their transit depending on the number of times they retrograde back into the previous sign. (Retrograde means when the rotation of the planet slows down to be exceeded by that of the earth and therefore appears to be moving backward.) When there are two or more phases (i.e., a planet entering the early degrees of a sign for a couple of months, retrograding backward into the end degrees of the previous sign, and then once again reentering the new sign), the second phase will often be the most important, and although there is no steadfast rule, it will usually be the time when that planet is felt most profoundly. However, because I want to keep the structure of this book simple, I am not going to go into the meanings of each phase of retrogradation. Instead, I will treat each planet's sojourn in a sign as a total experience, to be regarded for its creative and evolutionary potential.

Use this as a guide for reflection, to relive certain past experiences in your life in the light of a larger meaning. Likewise, use it as a creative aid to help you grow emotionally and spiritually in the present and future.

Finally, keep in mind that the older you become, potentially, the greater will be your experience and understanding and, likewise, the greater the possibility for making these planetary cycles positive creative periods that work for you.

Saturn Opposition Sun in Aries

This is a frustrating period when new structures must be built to support old ones that have ceased to function effectively. It is a time of testing whether your personal goals, values, and relationships may no longer hold the same meaning for you that they once did. The result is that you may feel forced to reevaluate your future and yourself.

Your exceptionally impatient nature may feel thwarted now. Emotionally, you may feel tense and anxious as disappointments arise and life seems to require more energy to get less accomplished. This is a time when the wheels of life are moving slowly, and sometimes there are a lot of petty problems caught in between. At moments you may feel deeply conflicted, irrationally fearful, depressed, and very tense. When this emotional strain gets out of control, it can become physical. Your health can suffer now, because your energy and vitality are low. Therefore, it is important to give your physical well-being the attention it deserves.

Your self-value is being tested now, and nagging doubts may worry you. This is a time when you question the meaning of many of the things you are doing. You may also feel inclined to criticize yourself when life becomes frustrating and troublesome. It is very important that you work on the areas of your life, the faults and habits, that are holding you back and diminishing your capacity to have a richer life. This is the period in which to build a firmer identity that you enjoy more fully. It is the time to create meaningful structures for your life that are so rich that they sustain you in times of self-doubt and crisis.

It is crucial now to do good things for yourself, things that are constructive emotionally, psychologically, physically, and spiritually. This is an important cycle of construction that occurs every seven years, and what you construct at this time will sustain you through the next cycle. This is the time to create a new self and a new self-image—perhaps through a diet, a new health plan, an exercise regime that makes you like yourself more because you stick to it. However, the changes on the physical level should only be the beginning.

If you are really going to thrive, as opposed to merely survive, it is essential that you work to develop your mind and spirit now. Saturn is the planet of work, and it forces us to move beyond ourselves. The richer your self is, the more you will enjoy yourself and the more you will have to fall back on.

It is likely that there will be times now when you feel so lackluster that there will be little that really interests you. Simple routines may become unbearably onerous, and the monotony of life will seem to be dragging you down. It is true that you are expending more energy now and getting less accomplished. However, persistence is required; patience must be developed; and existing structures and methods of organization in your life have to be reexamined.

The more efficient the structures you develop to accomplish the tasks you wish to accomplish, the easier your life will be and the less you will feel the sort of anxiety that just keeps coming at you. It is important to create your structures so that they work for you at maximum efficiency. Ideally, they should eliminate time-wasting situations and carry you along to where you want to be with less energy expended on your part.

It is important now not to allow the frustrations, disappointments, and overall aggravations usually associated with this transit to defeat you. At times you may feel like giving up and going to bed with a book. Effort may seem useless and your energy severely blocked. However, when you feel like this, keep in mind that it is leaden energy raining from the sky and is only temporary. There is a tomorrow and it will be brighter and more exciting. Keep believing in this as you move forward moment by moment. In the meantime, try to do everything positive that you can for yourself.

At times during this transit, fear and worry will consume you. If you are in a relationship, many of your frustrations will be vented in this area. You may find the habits or propensities of your partner unbearably frustrating, or you may worry irrationally about his or her health and well-being. On the other hand, it could also be that you feel consumed with a fear of abandonment. There will be moments when you feel cold, angry, moody, and completely turned off.

This is a very difficult transit for people in relationships for it seems to blacken their vision of life and the world and forces them to see only the flaws. Sometimes relationships break up as a result of this antagonistic undercurrent, which surfaces as apathy. It is important to face problems now, but to face them constructively. Effective communication is absolutely essential.

This is the time to create new ways of dealing with old problems. It is also important now to work on your way of expressing anger. It could be that the way you display it is exacerbating your conflicts with your partner. Anger that controls you now will affect both your emotional and physical well-being. Therefore, it is important to express yourself in a way that makes you like yourself.

As a catharsis, it would be helpful to begin to express yourself creatively now. Take up a musical instrument, try your hand at painting, write poems about your feelings, or even keep a daily journal of your thoughts—all of these activities could provide meaningful routes for probing the deeper reaches of yourself to discover new, richer layers of your consciousness. Taking a leaden depression and turning it into the golden experience of a poem—even if the poem is depressing—will give you something creative and positive, something more of yourself from a negative experience. From this small experience you will begin to expand yourself and in the process of exploring your deeper reaches, enjoy yourself.

This particular life cycle challenges you to grow beyond yourself, and this is not an easy challenge. However if you look at your frustrations as challenges that you *can* master and grow from and triumph through, you have the chance to turn this period into a succession of very rich learning experiences.

As a final note, it is important now not to depress yourself. When you do feel bad, concentrate on your strengths, not your flaws. Make a list of your attributes and read them over to yourself at least once a day. Then focus your willful attention on uncovering and discovering more of the interesting aspects of yourself. This will take work, but if you make it like a game, it can also be an entertaining, vital experience. Picture yourself as you would like to be ideally and develop that image in your mind. Eventually the bad period will pass and you will have yourself to thank for the new you. If you just try a little harder now, during the most difficult moments, you will eventually be a far more powerful person, enjoying your life and yourself endlessly.

Pluto Opposition Sun in Aries

Because Pluto is such a slow-moving planet, sitting in one sign for several years, its effect will often be a subtle one, affecting the deeper reaches of the emotions. The closer Pluto moves to the exact degree of an individual's sun sign, of course, the more pronouncedly will this influence be felt.

At its worst, this aspect has a separative effect and can end a relationship that has had serious problems simmering under its surface for quite some time. One of the partners may feel that finally the situation is spent, that it has run its course, and that it does not offer enough positive possibilities to be worth continuing. At the same time, there can be a tremendous amount of emotional ambivalence felt about actually making the final decision to sever it. Quite often with this particular opposition, situations appear to arise externally, apart from the will. Therefore, it can be that it is the other person who instruments the break, although the relationship has been the cause for much mutual suffering.

This sort of breakup can have a deathlike effect on the psyche, leaving the person feeling lost and completely uncentered. Here, the challenge is for a complete rebirth that will allow the individual more room to breathe and to grow.

Because Pluto is also the planet of renewal, relationships that break up now often seem to regenerate themselves; the people involved try to come back together to work out their problems and give it another try. If the mutual differences are too enormous, or if the reason for the revival of the relationship is really dependency, it is likely that this renewal will be only temporary. It is holding back at least one, if not both, people from expanding, and eventually this constriction will once again be felt in the consciousness and exacerbated until the drowning person finds the courage to let go.

Aries is usually an ambitious, independent sign, although this can be modified by other factors in the horoscope. Yet, underneath the independence there lurks a need for union that is more profound than in the other fire signs. Because of Libra on its natural seventh house cusp, Aries feels more complete with a partner. Yet often the problem is that being with a partner constricts an Aries's sense of spontaneous self-expression. Because there is this internal conflict, this transit period may prove more troublesome for this sign.

On the positive side, this could be a time of self-discovery through relationships. It could be a time when you realize that you can love a lot of people in a lot of different ways without compromising your center with a lot of emotional *Sturm und Drang*. Perhaps you will find that you can experience excitement in different kinds of ways, can enjoy different kinds of people, and have discovered different aspects of yourself. These are some of the rewards for meeting the challenge of this period, which is self-discovery through exploration. What you will find is that there is no end to yourself, your creativity, your sheer capacity for living. It is a time to test your own power and, in the process, to realize that you are more powerful than you originally thought.

All endings, now, herald new beginnings, and with

your inherent Ariean courage and spirit you will find a plethora of ways to move forward and celebrate the new.

This could be a time, however, when you feel more moody than usual. There may be moments when you feel that your sense of self is being drowned by painful oceanic emotions rising to the surface, triggered by difficult external situations. Perhaps you are not seeing objectively a situation in which your ego is involved. It could be that your stubborness is holding you back and reducing your possibilities. It could also be that your ego is telling you to hold on to a situation or circumstance that actually is in some way holding you back and diminishing your sense of self. Objectivity is crucial now, for your sense of self will suffer for anything that you do not see with dispassion.

A problem with the Aries personality is that they always have to be right. What you have to learn now is that winning a contest is not necessarily going to bring you the prize. There are certain contests that you should not even enter into with serious expectations, because the experience could be self-destructive. At the same time, hanging on could be self-destructive to the degree that you compromise your own sense of self-esteem.

An Aries who does not respect himself is a very depressed person. Unlike a lot of the other signs, your expectations are exceptionally high. You want a lot from life and from yourself, and if you do not win, you will either hate yourself or take it out on another person. If you do not think of life in terms of winning but rather of trying your best and just experiencing, in the long run, your life will be a lot easier and you will be a lot happier. Your challenge now is to learn how to trust yourself, and to trust that trust even if you fall. You always have the inherent grace to pick yourself up, and the world will admire you more than if you got it right the first time. Yours is a sign that can be very happy if you just allow yourself. Now is the time to do it, and to enjoy the power of the striving along the way.

Saturn Opposition Sun in Taurus

This is a difficult time of decreased vitality and increased responsibility. Saturn has a leaden vibration that permeates the mind and body until it weighs down the entire being.

Problems seem to be coming from other people now. Misunderstandings are in the air because the quality of communication is quite low. During this time you may feel victimized by other people's callousness. Authority figures may prove troublesome, and friends may impose themselves upon you in ways that you find emotionally unbearable. It is especially difficult for you to say no now because it is the nature of Saturn to make you feel guilty if you have not risen to excel in every situation.

You will find now that you have to rise up out of yourself and reach beyond yourself to accomplish what you want to accomplish. Your energy and vitality are low now, and there may be many mornings that you feel more like turning over than conquering the world. During this period you have to take care of your health—keep in mind that the feeling will pass and take life one step at a time.

Because you have, by nature, such a strong degree of patience, you will be able to endure this transit much more easily than a lot of other signs. However, the areas in which it is likely to hit you hardest are your ego and your relationships with people.

People of this sign need a lot of love and at the same

time are very insecure about their ability to attract it and maintain it. Because you care so much about the people in your life, all personal conflicts are particularly painful. Now is the time when you will feel especially compromised by them, and it will take all of your emotional effort to see to it that you are not taken advantage of.

If you have been in a difficult relationship, it is likely that it will end now. It is important to realize that this ending is not beyond your control but rather something that your self needs if it is going to grow in a vital manner. It is likely that for a long time you have been neglecting your own needs in order to fulfill the fantasies of your partner, maintaining the relationship chiefly for security. In doing so, an important part of you has been stifled, and it is likely that for some time now you have been feeling a strain. If your relationship ends now, it is a sign that you have been giving up too much of yourself in your effort to maintain what you have. The price you have been paying, for your inner freedom, was so high that it was costing your happiness. Under Saturn we suffer dearly for our security needs. Its lesson is that we have to trust ourselves enough emotionally to move forward, rather than sitting on ourselves in fear. Anyone who has successfully passed through the tests of Saturn has moved past the concepts of both security and insecurity and has learned how to go inside, to the best of his or her self, and bring out whatever is needed to master the situation.

If, despite effort, the situation cannot be mastered, then this person has the courage to trust that in the long run it is all for the best and ultimately some better opportunity or circumstance will come along.

This kind of trust is especially difficult for the Taurean nature, which is so practical and earthbound, forever seeking reassurance and emotional collateral, always concentrating on long-term returns. Distrust is intrinsic to this nature, which fears that its hopes will fall through at the very last minute. However, Saturn demands that we begin to look at our life in the short-term, and if we are open enough, it shows us that this perspective has its own reward.

There will be disappointments now that will force you to face the materialization of your fears, and through these experiences you can gain new perspectives. Very often when life situations fall apart, the pain and panic that they create have little to do with the ultimate reality of the situation. Many times it is possible to look back and say it was just as well that that did not happen, because if it did, then this could never have happened.

The Saturn cycle is a frustrating period. It will be a challenge to look at life in such a manner and to try to learn a liberating, growth-producing lesson from every frustration and disappointment. At times you will simply have to wait out certain things. Unimagined obstacles may crop up now. On the other hand, it is also possible to change your perspective on a situation to the point that you can manipulate obstacles and make them work for you. When this is impossible, you must not cling to your loss. Move on to what you feel is more satisfying, and develop the attitude that one day things will be much better. Unless you are a particularly negative person, you know, from experience, that this is always true.

Much of life may seem like a burdensome responsibility now. You want to feel lighter and less serious about the various elements in your life, and one day you will. Try to see your problems with greater dispassion. One way to do this is to divert yourself by becoming involved with the problems of someone else. This is always an excellent self-forgetting technique and beats going to bed, because it can make you feel more worthwhile afterward.

Through all of the disappointments and difficulties you are suffering now, it is advisable to keep in mind that everyone at times has problems that seem insurmountable to them. This may seem to be an obvious, platitudinous statement. However, the fact is that when we are hit with a loss serious enough to constitute a personal crisis, the first, and perhaps continuing, impulse is to feel we are alone in a world where everyone else is happy and everyone else is loved. The truth is that the person who has never experienced maddening frustration, terrible fear, or heartrending crisis is rare indeed. These experiences are part of what life is all about and are inescapable.

The critical element is the attitude that one maintains in the face of each frustration and disappointment. Our attitudes are our highways to greater inner freedom. And when we are free on the inside, we are no longer controlled by what is happening on the outside.

The challenge during this period is to confront and experience your own fears and move beyond them. Do not allow them to confine or define you. Dwell in that positive part of yourself that you like best and enlarge it daily. Keep a journal of your progress in dealing more successfully with life. Record the events, and the changes you are going through now, and then write down what you think you can learn from each experience. Then in another section write down your thoughts and your feelings and all the things that you have learned. Not only will this help you through a difficult time, but when you read back to yourself what you have written, you will be utterly amazed at how much you have grown and have become richer from the experience. Consequently, you will also enjoy and respect yourself that much more.

You must learn to respect your highest faculties now, despite the voice of nagging doubt. Keep on trying *despite* all obstacles, and one day you will become the power of your own striving, and a life force deep inside of you will reign supreme.

Uranus Opposition Sun in Taurus

This is a time of profound psychological change that will manifest in your life very slowly. New feelings are growing within you now, and old fears may be erupting and dying off.

Change is something that does not come comfortably to your Taurean nature, and this is a life cycle that is at least culminating in change.

Old habits, fears, limitations, and empty relationships are falling to the wayside now. There will be moments when the change will be abrupt and perhaps uncomfortable. At times you may feel tempted to associate it with loss. However, the important thing to keep in mind is that any situation that ends now, should end. Although you may be holding on fiercely, what you are holding onto is holding you back from becoming more.

On the other hand, new conditions are also creating themselves, whether or not you are consciously aware of the seeds of the new beginning. Emerging now are unexplored aspects of yourself that encompass new needs, desires, and feelings that will move your life in new directions.

A significant area in which this will be felt is the area of love and friendship. Perhaps you are realizing now that the two should be tied together. New people will be entering your life, and you will be forming new kinds of relationships. On a positive level, this could be a time when you marry or quite unexpectedly meet a grand love. Many astrologers feel that a relationship formed under a Uranus opposition will not last due to its impulsive quality. However, this is governed far more by the individual's level of maturity and degree of consciousness than by the nature of the aspect.

The changes you make in your life now are important, for they will set the tone and the quality of your future. This is a time when your entire identity is transforming. Perhaps you are becoming secure enough to see yourself more as you would like to be seen. Old fears are rising up and then falling by the wayside as you slowly confront and master them. Up until now you have been doing what you should have been doing. Now things will begin to pay off, and your life will eventually start to look the way you have always wanted it to. That means you have created positive new experiences by manipulating the changes to their most constructive advantage.

If you have been in a long-term relationship, you may find yourself reevaluating aspects of it. It may be that your partner has been fulfilling old aspects of yourself that now are less vital. At the same time, your security needs have probably remained the same. This conflict between your need for change versus your need for stability could be a problematic one.

If your partner does not grow along with you now, underlying tensions could develop that you are not even conscious of. The deepest part of you is seeking a richer quality of experience, defined by a generative love based on the ideals of friendship.

This is an important time of becoming. It is a time to move beyond the confine of previous structures where you were merely passing time and repeating experience. You must multiply yourself now. If you are to benefit greatly, you must abandon yourself to the effort.

Some very important changes may manifest in your

career now. Old conditions could be ending. At the same time, new opportunities that you have been wanting for some time may materialize.

Essentially, the archetypal meaning of this period is ultimate gain from the restructuring of self and life. It is a time of endings and exciting new beginnings; a time of becoming acquainted with new aspects of yourself that you never knew existed. It is also a time to try to love more freely, without fear.

Pluto Opposition Sun in Taurus

Pluto is the slowest moving planet and has an equally slow evolutionary effect upon the consciousness. Unconscious drives, needs, and compulsions are coming to the surface now, and the result can often be painful. Pluto's effect on the sun is to instill identity crises that provoke personal tests of power. There is often a sense of profound ego-frustration with this transit, and because of the nature of the opposition, intense personal relationships are usually the catalysts.

Sometimes these relationships will involve a compulsive love-tie—an on-and-off again situation that keeps renewing itself. This kind of relationship always involves, for one partner, a sacrifice of the self, along with a diminished sense of ego, to maintain the tie. The other partner usually has a complex psychological, often sexual, hold that involves some form of punishment along with the satisfactions received.

Under this transit there could also be a complicated problem with a person in authority whose behavior appears to be unjust. This kind of situation usually involves an intense ego clash that also compromises the sense of self. Usually these situations end painfully, with the rage lingering on in the mind long after the situation is over.

When the rage is particularly intense, it is often because some unacceptable trait in the self is reflected in the other person. This is a terribly difficult thing to see and perhaps even more difficult to admit. However, this is a time when you have the opportunity to become acquainted with new aspects of yourself through the catalyst of personal conflict. Power struggles of all kinds are prevalent now, and in each one of them is a liberating lesson to be learned about your own psyche. The more you understand yourself, the more inner control you will have over yourself and, consequently, over the externals in your life.

This is a time when you may find that you are more blindly driven to achieve a certain goal for the purpose of asserting your personal power. During this cycle, very subtly but increasingly, power will become an issue that permeates many of your life considerations. Your need to feel the manifestation of it in your life is greater than ever now. At times this will bring you emotional problems because you will associate your identity with your mastery of your material conditions.

This could be a very dangerous tendency because intrinsic to the Taurus nature is a deeply suppressed feeling of worthlessness. It is the unconscious conviction that you don't really deserve that creates many limiting situations in your life. It is the propensity of the Taurean nature to try almost too hard, as an overcompensation for the lack of self-worth, and then to feel deeply grateful for the result that you have created. When things fall through for you, as they do for everybody, you feel uniquely shamed and are so hard on yourself that it borders on self-punishment. Moralism and a sense of justice are intrinsic to your nature. You want to get only what you deserve, but when you are not really convinced that you do deserve, not only are you going to be disappointed and passed over, but some person who may not deserve anything, but who firmly believes that they do, will most definitely succeed where you have "failed." Desperately you want the world to be fair, and because of this many times you have been cruelly disappointed. Not only is the world not fair, it operates according to one basic rule: He who is convinced that he deserves gets what he wants regardless of the degree of substance of his worth.

This is something you have to seriously think about now, for issues of justice and worth will increasingly be coming to the forefront. Every disappointment and frustration is an opportunity to take serious stock of yourself and to begin to look at yourself in a new way. Your challenge during this cycle is to be kinder to yourself, to learn to be more self-accepting, and to see yourself through the prism of loyalty and kindness rather than rage or resentment. Your personal life can be exactly the way you want it to be. But first you have to learn to trust yourself and to be less hard on yourself when things do not happen as you would like them to.

Hitler was a Taurus. The inferiority that he projected upon the Jews was his own sense of inferiority that had become consciously unbearable for him. He is a very extreme case of the potential destructiveness that an unaffirmed self is capable of.

Intrinsic to the Taurus nature is a strong degree of tenacity and determination, which is a very positive trait. However, when this determination becomes blind and controlling, it can carry you very far away from your center. At this point, the choices that you begin to make, are born out of compulsion rather than wisdom. The result is that your behavior may begin to have an undermining effect upon your intention to do the best.

What you will have to learn during the difficult moments now are that grit, determination, and game plans are not all that is needed to get you successfully through life. You also have to develop a more affirmative sense of self that sustains you even during the bad times.

Many people enter psychotherapy during Pluto transits of their sun sign because the sun symbolizes our sense of identity and Pluto often brings about situations that cloud it out and cause painful confusion. It is not uncommon under this transit to lose sight of who you thought you were and to feel at a loss to understand how to get that positive sense of self back. There is often a deep loneliness of the soul experienced during this period, charcterized by an inability to connect meaningfully with others. What is in fact happening is that the psychological changes that the self is evolving through are dimming a healthy affirmative self-awareness, and if we cannot connect with ourselves, the mind to the heart, it is also impossible to connect meaningfully with others.

Many different conditions that have lost their psychological value die off under the influence of Pluto. Stale friendships and empty marriages that have become based merely on security finally come to an end. These endings are not sudden and shocking, however, and have really been brewing under the surface for a very long time. Pluto is the planet of death and regeneration. Its lesson is that inherent to each deathlike situation is an elevating rebirth, if we can keep our hearts open long enough to be able to receive it. However, the problem with the grudge-bearing Taurus nature is that with the experience of pain there is a strong propensity to kill off emotional response altogether. When we cut off our hearts, though, we also cut off the life inside us and no growth and wisdom can be gained.

This is a time when you must try to free yourself of your lower-ego power needs and see your life in a larger perspective in order to gain the wisdom that will bring you to a new source of power within yourself. Taurus is ruled by the planet Venus, the planet of love. Love is your nature and when you cut off your ability to love, to feel, to care about yourself and those closest to you, you have become a very dark and depressed person.

If you feel dark and depressed during this transit, as many people do, it is because you are approaching yourself and your life in the wrong way. Your values, life-style, and perhaps relationships, are failing to nurture your inner being. New choices have to be made around the issue of meaning, rather than material power. New paths have to be forged and problems grappled with in a new way. Life cannot continue to be looked at through the sole perspective of win and lose, rich and poor, power and powerlessness. Situations and relationships have to be able to give you a quality of meaning or they will bring you nothing but a sense of emptiness and anxiety.

However, before you can even consider your relationship to the workings of the world around you, in order to find peace and joy, you must stop and look at your relationship with yourself. If you are unhappy, ask yourself why you are being unnecessarily hard on yourself, why you drive yourself to the point where you feel dead inside, why you inflict a deep sense of shame upon yourself when you fail to live up to your own goals, why you distrust the people that you want to love you, why you are convinced that you don't really deserve the love, joy, happiness that you see in the lives of others.

If your answer to any of these questions was nebulous, then you have serious work to do. You specifically must learn how to give yourself love. Begin by doing good things for yourself that are constructive and enhance your sense of well-being. Then make a list of all of the special qualities you have that you secretly enjoy. List everything you can think of as an accomplishment and every wonderful personal characteristic, one of which I will give you—the ability to care and love. See that loving Taurus ability as something that will set you apart from other, colder, selfish people, as a person who is remembered warmly in the hearts of many, as a person whose integrity inspires the deepest loyalty. This quality alone is so overwhelmingly generative that if you make your mind connect with the inherent beauty of your heart and affirm it daily, your life will change and you will be able to become practically anything that you want to be.

This is a time of profound and potentially highly meaningful change. First the inner part of you will change, and at times it will be painful, but if you continue to affirm yourself *in spite of*, eventually your outer life will also change only for the better. But, as a very simple basic, you must learn how to exercise self-love. Whenever something disappointing happens in your life, see it as a learning experience and search within yourself to find the wisdom to help you to grow brighter. And whenever you fear or feel bad about yourself, STOP and discipline your mind to see the issue from the exact opposite perspective, which is affirmative. Remind yourself several times daily, *every* day, of your unique worth as an individual. Concentrate on it. Hold it in your mind. Go to sleep with it. Trust that one day in the future you will look back at yourself and see a stranger.

Uranus Opposition Sun in Gemini

This is an unpredictable period in which anything can happen and the completely unexpected is the norm. Your Gemini need for mental control will be tested now as your life, self, psyche, and relationships undergo sudden, abrupt changes that may leave you feeling a bit chaotic. You may feel more nervous, high-strung, restless, impatient, and irritable now. On the deepest levels of your being, you will feel the need for change, for freedom from stagnant life-patterns, habits, situations, and relationships that are no longer vital. The degree to which you resist making positive changes or rigidly fear the situations coming about is the degree to which you will experience tension and nervousness.

During this period you may feel anxious about being closed in, confined, limited, in any way. A lot of old habits may be holding you back now, and it is conceivable that you are projecting these anxieties onto your relationships. This is a time when you may find yourself having problems with someone in authority who in some way is cramping your style. Regardless of your convictions, it would be most constructive to keep the lines of communication open while you try to maintain your objectivity.

In general, this is an important weeding-out period. However, although friendships and relationships may end now, others will be born unexpectedly to replace them. During this transit you will attract what you dwell upon. Therefore, it is important to be positive in your thoughts, actions, and reactions.

You should make a strenuous effort now to live your life more fluidly and not desiccate the quality of your experiences with your mind. There will be moments when irritations and antagonisms challenge your sense of well-being. Therefore, you will have to develop greater emotional elasticity to be able to put your problems in perspective.

It is a particular Gemini characteristic to create problems where they need not exist by looking on the negative side of life. This is a time when you will pay heavily for these emotional constraints with extreme nervousness and bouts of high-strung behavior. At times you may feel forced to surrender your will to the flow of a situation. However, you have the potential now of gaining a much deeper trust in yourself. Ideally, you will emerge from this period with a serenity and self-detachment born from the experience of having faced and conquered your deepest fears. However, first you must work through your passive resistance to change and your tendency to think that the world owes you something.

The entire direction of your life could change dramatically under this transit. Job, profession, marriage, love life—any or all of these areas could bring unexpected problems of possibilities, depending on the positivity of your mind. If you think "big" now, you will see a sense of possibility in every problem. At this point, the spark of potential in each new experience should replace fear and the self-created strictures of good and bad.

The lesson to be learned now is to view your life and yourself in freer ways that are dynamic, creative, and constructive. Life offers endless possibilities once you get beyond the diminishing strictures of your own mind. The only thing holding you back now is your own resignation. This is the time to distinguish your fears from realistic limitations and to push yourself harder to realize the dreams that can become your life.

Neptune Opposition Sun in Gemini

The positive aspect of this transit has to do with the challenge to you to express your creativity. This means not only writing, or some other artistic endeavor but, equally important, your life, how you live it and the quality of the choices that you make.

The vibrations of Neptune have to do with nebulousness, the sort of nebulousness that can range from artistic inspiration to emotional confusion. This sort of confusion happens to be your nemesis to begin with. You have a tendency to suffer from circular thinking and to create problems where they do not exist. Under this transit, in very subtle ways, you may suffer more emotionally from the illusions that you embrace. At the same time, you stand to benefit greatly from all the creative choices you make *and execute* in the area of self-expansion.

You pay heavily now for false idealism. That is not to say that you should not be positive in your thinking. However, you should also be realistic, because your illusions will undermine you. Any new ventures entered into now should be thought out carefully. Legal problems could arise and partnerships of all kinds may extract some sort of sacrifice on your part.

This is a time when you might be wrestling with an old love that is alternately dissolving and rekindling itself. There is a quality to this experience that requires some sort of sacrifice from you. Depending on the situation, this is not necessarily bad. It could be that this sacrifice has helped you to grow up, and because of it you are less narcissistic and worthy of greater emotional responsibility. On the other hand, if the other person is only taking from you selfishly, it is time to reevaluate your ties to him or her as well as your need for such a masochistic situation. Often, Geminis have such a deep-seated fear of intimacy that they can only become involved with a distant person who does not give them anything emotionally. If you are caught in this bind and it is restricting your potential and capacity for emotional fulfillment, it might be wise to consider psychotherapy. It is not necessary to endure the bondages you unwillingly place upon yourself. Remember that we all have them and we all must work assiduously to relieve ourselves of them.

The greater the degree of your own emotional confusion, the more susceptible you will be now to disappointment in love. Notice that I am predicating this disappointment on the degree of your self-knowl-edge, *not on the fate of the stars.* The people who come into your life now will reflect the nature of your own consciousness. If you are lonely and are continually disappointed in your love life, it is because you are frightened, confused, and do not trust your higher self to attract the love that you desire. It could very well be that you say that you want a relationship, but at the same time you are terrified of what that commitment might entail, and you won't be honest with yourself about the conflict.

On the other hand, thinking positively, if you have worked to gain self-knowledge (and all Geminis need to work on self-knowledge), the people who enter your life now could be uniquely creative, spiritual, or in some way highly inspirational. It is up to you to make sure that anyone that you come to trust with your deeper feelings is not unstable, irresponsible, or untrustworthy.

This is an important time to build a more creative approach to life. Mood swings may temporarily undermine you now, but far less so if you have a rich inner life. If you do not have a rich inner life, it is a time to create one. It is a time to stop running around in an effort to escape yourself and to try staying home and reading. Through books, discover new interests that in the next few years you can explore. Try keeping a journal of your thoughts; it may eventually lead to a larger writing project that you might find fulfilling. Explore a philosophy that will increase the meaning of your life. The greatest philosophers were also brilliant psychologists who wrestled painfully and personally with the human dilemma to find answers that we all can benefit from. Therefore, it is wise, in a moment of despair to call upon them.

All of these alternatives will ease a tendency now toward depression which could range from an oceanic sense of isolation, to the dull pain of an identity crisis that does not seem to resolve itself. You must be reminded that all the answers are already inside you, even if they do not come through as quickly as you would desire. Once you relax and begin to trust yourself, they will all come through, and you will one day look back at yourself and smile.

A familiar feeling that very often occurs under the influence of a Neptune transit is that nothing is ever enough. The quality of life leaves a lot to be desired, and the quality of your love life does not measure up to your expectations. The challenge under this transit is to stop complaining and do something about it. One particular Gemini person sublimated a very painful year and profound emotional disappointment by writing her first novel as she completed all the course work for her doctorate in philosophy! Not only did she surprise herself by trying that much harder, she also came away feeling proud of herself in a way that she had never dreamed of. By courageously confronting the feeling that her life was not enough and accepting the challenge by *doing something about it*, she made it become more than she ever thought possible.

Ideally, this could be a time when everyone explores their own creative and philosophic boundaries. To stagnate now is the worst choice you can make for yourself, because time itself is possibility. As Camus once said, "Every healthy creature tends to multiply himself." This kind of health is necessary for the richest kind of happiness, which conflict and struggle cannot deny, but merely postpone. Trust this in the most trying of times and your life will eventually become the sort of dream that is never marred by illusion.

Saturn Square the Sun in Cancer

This is a time of tests—personal, emotional, psychological—the sum challenge of which is to grow past the painful emotional limitations that you impose upon yourself.

Cancer is a deeply emotional, supersensitive sign that often suffers inwardly because of its tendency to brood and hold back powerful feelings. It is not uncommon for these feelings to make you ill physically. The motivation behind such self-protectiveness is a bone-deep sense of insecurity and a free-floating sense of fear. Saturn is the planet associated with fear. By hard aspect in transit, its electromagnetic energies stimulate our unconscious to bring us in acute contact with our fears and to impose them on the happenings of the external world.

It is this omnivorous fearfulness that seriously holds this sign back from fully enjoying life. The symbol associated with Cancer is the crab, and just like the crab, there is a retreat back into the shell whenever the world poses what appears to be a threat. Cancers nurse slights and lick wounds out of utter subjectivity. Because of this subjectivity, it is a profound problem for the Cancer individual to get beyond himself or herself, and just as great a problem for another individual to get in, as well.

The transit of Saturn is challenging your subjectivity now. The problems and emotional conflicts you experience now will give you the opportunity to give up something of yourself that you no longer need—and that is your emotional baggage.

The baggage of the Cancer consciousness is that it makes its life far more complicated than need be. This is the time to see that truth through the prism of the problems in your life. Saturn will make you suffer now for all of your negative thinking. The only way to make the depressive moods stop is to begin to change your attitudes.

Saturn is moving through your solar fourth house now, challenging your need for security. The fourth house is the house of the home and also of the soul and the soul needs. That deepest part of you may feel frustrated now. There may be emotional problems or conflicts with a marriage, relationship, or family situation. What these conflicts will reveal is a block in your psyche that is preventing you from releasing yourself from the confining situation. Saturn in the fourth often indicates the feeling of soul sickness, and when it squares the sun, this is played out through a compromised sense of self that diminishes the extent of your achievements.

If you feel a terrible soul pain now, there are things that you are not allowing yourself to see and you are therefore falling victim to them. Cancers often choose to be martyrs as their unique form of self-diminishment. Women often give of themselves to the degree that they have no self left, and afterward are bitterly resentful. The men, on the other hand, are so insecure that they often don't give at all. Consequently, they are hurt and angry when the women they want most have the courage to walk away. There are serious lessons to be learned now in giving. We should give if we care. However, you cannot really give of yourself if you do not have a self. Further, giving so much of yourself that you diminish yourself is evil for both you and the other person.

I define evil here as anything that is severely out of balance. Such a lack of balance, if it is not adjusted accordingly, is certain to bring pain and suffering. Saturn squaring in the sign of Cancer is saying simply, get balanced with your emotions, with the inner and the outer you, between what you give and what you take, between what you give and what you expect to get back, and finally between your emotional needs and your ego-identity. All of your suffering exists because you set up unbalanced situations. Start to look coldly at your life and see it with objectivity. If you can only see it subjectively, which means viewing *only* the negative results of your choices, you will suffer the deep depression of self-diminishment. In addition to that, it is highly likely that you will also make yourself sick. Ulcers, stomach problems, nervous problems, and corrosive diseases of all kinds, are common to natives of this sign because their emotional behavior is corrosive.

The giving aspect of Cancer is a tricky one and often it is an impulse born far less out of generosity than of an insecure need to buy affection. Underlying this is a belief that affection and loyalty can be bought by behavior. First mistaken assumption. However, underlying this belief is the more insidious belief that anything you get, you have to pay for.

The truth is that emotional things require a price only if we are guilty enough to believe that we have to pay a price. Change your attitude and watch all the prices disappear. Naturally, this is not such an easy undertaking. However, you must begin to realize that you set up the situations where you always turn out the victim. And that *can* be changed if you want it to be.

Saturn is the planet associated with the principle of restriction. When it transits in hard aspect to the sun or asscendant, it says you must rescind the limitations you impose upon yourself or else your reality will become all of those limitations manifested as external problems.

Its wisdom is that life does not have to be that way, and it should not be. However, until we begin to learn through our painful mistakes, life will continue to reinforce our expectations of suffering. The lessons of Saturn experienced during this life cycle are portals of self-liberation. If you do not wallow around in the tears that you have created, your life can change and you can create what you want.

Intrinsic to this sign is a definite streak of masochism that must be worked through. Cancer men are attracted to cold, selfish, dominant women who walk all over them. This is because there is a psychological transference to the power that these women project, which the Cancer man does not feel inside of his sensitive little ego. I mean "little" literally, because this type of choice is due to a very poor sense of self that may be compensated for in all kinds of ways. The women are woeful hangers-on who are often attracted to the most selfish of men. Again, because of the lack of sense of self that the Cancer woman feels within her deepest reaches.

Therefore, regardless of what events are occurring on the outside now, the origin of all the problems goes back to the lack of a conscious center or core. When this sign remains largely unconscious, it is the moodiest and the most easily victimized. For the life choices are confused and born from hunger, fear, or anger rather than from some self-affirmative motivation. Until the Cancer individual develops a healthy sense of self and is able to first give itself the love that it is seeking from the outside, it will treat its close emotional relationships as if they were food. The unfortunate others will feel consumed by need, guilt, or resentment. This will ultimately have a separative effect, with the Cancer person on the apparent losing end. The end of the circle is greater anger and ultimately greater hunger.

What Saturn is saying now is take a courageous look at your life and have the courage to see what is there and what is really holding you back as opposed to what appears to be. Have the courage to cut loose from your victim role and start to learn the enjoyment of being master of your own life. What that means specifically is coming to realize that you are somebody, and somebody *significant*, that you must give love to. Do good things for yourself. Learn how to make yourself happy. Do not wait for it to come from the outside and then get angry with it does not. Be active now! Do not passively wait for Mr. or Ms. Right to come along or for your spouse to change or for your children to fulfill your expectations. YOU fulfill your own expectations of what you want life to be. YOU should be the one to decide. YOU are the one who is important!

If you are in emotional pain now, take a large white index card and write on it the following:

1. THE PAIN I FEEL NOW EXISTS BECAUSE I HAVE DIMINISHED MY OWN POWER AND WILL BY PLACING THEM IN SOMETHING OUTSIDE OF ME.

2. However, all the power I need is here, right now, inside of me.

3. I will concentrate one-pointedly on that power in my center and eventually become that power.

4. When I become that power, I will attract only the most positive experiences to me. Eventually I will become joy.

Read this affirmation to yourself daily as often as you can. Eventually your life will change, and you will no longer be concerned with what significant others think. That is because you will know. And you will know wisely.

Pluto Square the Sun in Cancer

The essential meaning of this life cycle is the challenge of self-ownership—the responsibility that entails and the potential freedom. Security bastions are challenged now and the message is that you must develop a sturdier, more secure sense of self that is sustaining.

Intrinsic to the Cancer nature is a propensity for losing the self to or in other people. Cancer is a highly security oriented sign that will diminish the self in order to establish situations of security to which it assigns power.

The degree to which you do that now is the degree to which you will make yourself suffer, on many levels. The challenge of this period is to face the death of old dependencies and the rebirth of a more affirmative sense of self. Pluto is in your fourth house now, challenging the foundations upon which you have structured your life. If these foundations are not benefiting you, they will begin to crumble and your sense of identity along with them. "Secure" relationships that may have functioned like shelters will suffer painful rumblings now. The longer you refuse to assertively take charge of your life, the longer you will be controlled by what is happening on the outside.

Emotionally speaking, Cancer is a sign that tends to wait for things to happen rather than assertively controlling the situations that most disturb it. In doing so, it often becomes a victim of the situations that it most wants to feel nurtured by. This feeling of victimization is particularly damaging, for it diminishes your sense of the power and the possibility that exists within you. The essence of this life cycle is that you will be going through emotional changes now that will give you the opportunity to recognize a new power.

At times now you may feel turbulent and terrified in the face of changes that may feel like more than you can cope with emotionally. However, these situations are really catalyzing your ability to reach beyond self-imposed limitations to become a person of greater magnitude. You must go within yourself now to see yourself as an individual who has power. The conflicts that are coming about at this time are because of your resistance to your own power. Therefore, you must stop waiting for another person or persons to better a bad situation and instead take the situation into your own hands to master it.

Pluto is the planet of destruction, rebirth, and transformation. In order for something to be transformed, it must also be broken down and reformed. That is where your life is now. Old structures, choices, behavioral patterns, and relationships are no longer working and must be reborn in the light of your potential as a human being. Because of your tendency to cling, the dying off will be painful. However, to the degree that you can make yourself see this as an exciting reconstruction period offering infinite possibility, you can get beyond your own anguish. This is not only the time to create a new sense of self, but also a freedom for that sense of self. The challenge is to see yourself as one who is master of his own kingdom. You must look to yourself for what you want, and you must find within yourself the strength and the uniqueness to create it. This is the time to plant within yourself the seeds of your highest hopes and to cultivate them with the most positive attitudes and tenacity. You are a bridge now, in a bridge of time, and you must go over that bridge, rather than getting stuck underneath it. Regardless of what is ending on the outside, you must understand that in yourself there are no stopping points. Your life is as rich as your mind will allow it to be and as wide as your courage will take it.

Think of this life cycle as one of serious becoming, and in your dark moments, do the following visualization.

Whether you are at home, at work, or simply walking down the street, see the sun radiating from your solar plexus. Feel its heat pressing outward and filling you up with feeling, and see the rays emanating up into your head and down into your feet. Associate your innermost being with this radiance. Then see that center grow brighter and brighter with the whitest light. Impose upon that white light a very clear image of what you want, and try to hold that image in your mind as you go about your tasks of the day.

If you do this visualization assiduously, eventually your life will change because your mind will have changed. At this point, your wish will materialize. Start to become acquainted now with the power within you to make positive changes materialize. Rise out of your own chaos and give birth to the rising sun that is within you. The power of the sun is you as long as you can make yourself see it. Remember this and you will control your own life. Forget it and you will dwell in darkness.

Saturn Square the Sun in Leo

The challenge during this period is to face the superficial values that you cling to, or worse, that you have let your life become. Saturn demands that we look at our lives, ourselves, and our relationships more seriously and in greater depth. It challenges the superficial structures that the ego tends to invest itself in, and it plays games of meaning with the mind.

Under the influence of Saturn, many things appear shallow and meaningless because they, in fact, are. Life seems full of obstacles and postponements. You may feel frustrated, discontent, and more impatient than ever to see the rewards of your efforts.

This is a time when you will tend to compare yourself to other people, and when you do, you may feel slighted by life. Your temptation to look to other people arises because you are not seeing the wonderful qualities in yourself. If you have been living merely on the material plane, this is a time when you will feel unhappy with yourself and your life because nothing material will sustain you emotionally. Emotionally and sexually you may feel cold, and mentally you may feel overworked and drained of your *joie de vivre*. The rhythm of life may take on a dull, demanding monotony as you feel oppressed by career pressures, anxious to your depths, and limited in your freedom. You may also feel deeply insecure, that your performance is on the line and that your power is being tested.

This is a time in which to become acquainted with

your real power, the power of your higher self. Any pain that you feel now is because you are diminishing your own unique power to by placing it in another person or situation. However, there is also a radiant power deep inside of you, and that is your capacity for all kinds of love.

This is more difficult to feel now because under a Saturn transit, your emotional vitality is at its lowest point. This is a fearful time, when you are excessively self-conscious and prone to diminish your self-approval to gain the approval of people lesser than you. Keep in mind that when you do, you will also come away feeling like less.

Now is the time to try very hard not to care about what others think or say, but to go by the deepest, most affirmative feelings in your heart. If you are surrounded by negative, insensitive people who diminish your sense of possibility, try to create and maintain an unfaltering perspective on your own self-worth. Get beyond surface problems and go deep inside yourself to see the possibility that is really there. Then make your decisions from that perspective.

Your propensity now will be to be very hard on yourself, and you must do the opposite. You must give yourself the love and the approval that you are seeking from the outside. As a measure of self-defense you must react less with your ego. Withdraw emotionally from situations that are making you a mere reactor and thereby compromising your personal freedom. Create your own safe space where you can contemplate the issues of your life with some degree of emotional balance which will bring you to the wisdom that is already within you.

Your need for material power and approval can often make you forget the thing that is most important in life and that is your capacity to love so many things.

Archetypically, Leo is a highly spiritual sign because it is the sign of spirit. When the spirit is developed, feeling is experienced on a level that is transpersonal and elevating. The nature of life is that painful problems always arise. However, instead of viewing them with panic and crushing anxiety, there is another higher, wiser part of the self to call upon, which looks down upon the problems that have to be solved as if from a mountain top. This doesn't alter the reality of what is happening at the moment. But it means that instead of being defined or diminished by the situation, one is, in a sense, above it. From this emotional perspective one is able to transcend the creaturely feeling of helplessness that can make life seem hopeless and utterly absurd.

A key to getting closer to your higher nature now is flexibility. This is extremely difficult for you because of your rigid compulsion to perform. However, what you will find is that blindly driving yourself in a bad situation will not only fail to master it but also make you more brittle and set up greater resistance to solving the problem. What you have to do now is something that you may not be able to do, and that is let go. Forget your ego and what you may think you look like from the outside and what you may think others are thinking about you, and try letting go of what is causing you pain. Give in and give yourself up as if you had taken a tranquilizer and nothing seemed so crucial anymore. The second that you do this successfully, you will have grown in consciousness and will have the strength of a greater wisdom to deal with the problem. Consequently, it will lose much of its awesomeness, and you will gain in spiritual power, which is the only real power.

When you gain in wisdom and you master this mental flexibility, shifting your weight mentally back and forth between what you do to perform versus the highest love and peace that you can feel in your heart, you will come to understand true power. True power is not ego power. Ego power assigns power to states outside the self, thereby diminishing the self, for there is always going to be someone who is more beautiful, more wealthy, more successful, and more privileged. Ego power works only while one is still winning. However, when age, death, or loss come on the scene, the person who has only ego power is in for a crisis, for the props on the outside simply do not ease the pain of a darkened self on the inside. The props do not change the wrinkles of the flesh and they can not deny the experience of death. At this point, the mind becomes a blackened battleground of the soul, and there is no apparent way out. One has to face up to the inner self and whatever one has chosen that to be.

However, when the spirit of a person is fully developed, neither the age of the body nor death can affect his or her true being. This is an individual that most people will never encounter in an entire lifetime. Regardless of the age or the physical appearance, they have a presence of such magnitude that there is an awesome radiance that shines forth. This is true power, and it is also the potential of the Leo nature, the sign of Spirit.

Alchemize each darkened experience now by finding the gold in it. Let the natural love of life that you have within you grow until the darkness of the material world is so far beneath you that you view it as if from a plane. See yourself in that plane. From the window you look out among the clouds and you become their peace. Soon you will land. Your feet will walk upon the earth and with the sky still in your heart you will feel the best that the earth has to offer. Enjoy it, but don't limit yourself to that alone. Keep in mind that you can have the sky, too, as soon as you see yourself as the sun.

Uranus Square the Sun in Leo

Uranus is the planet of change, and when it moves into a square of the sun sign, the unconscious need for change is sometimes experienced through the framework of conflict. However, when the consciousness is developed, this is an exciting time when you try new things and begin to live your life more creatively.

For the average person, this period is one of increased restlessness and perhaps irritability. You may find now that you are utterly impatient with anything or anyone who slows you down or gets in your way. Stagnant situations and people bore you more than ever now and instill you with the urge to leave it all behind.

Now you want illumination, stimulation, and excitement from your contacts. You want to meet new people, and you want to expand through your association with them. At this time you should consider constructive life changes that will bring you a greater sense of freedom and inner meaning.

It could very well be that you are going through a divorce or relationship breakup now. The release of this union will free you to become a different, more expansive person. It will also give you the freedom to master new goals. Deep inside, you may feel released from a lot of fear and anxiety that you have been carrying around for years. Maybe some of your fears have come true, but you have lived through them and triumphed, gaining a more positive sense of self.

You should know yourself better now. However, what is even more exciting is that you are also in a state of discovery. Ideally, there are many new things you want to accomplish and experience. Now you feel equal to conquering new challenges because you have struggled to master a number of conflicts in yourself.

One of those conflicts has to do with love. Love is always something of a problem for the Leo nature, for although the need to experience love is strong, there is an equally strong need for freedom, which the structures of relationships often seem to compromise. You are attracted to a different kind of person now, one who promises a new sense of freedom and possibility. Under this transit it is possible to meet such a person. However, the problem is that you may not feel ready to meet them and, therefore, may find ways to distance yourself from the situation. This is a time of intense emotional ambivalence. On one level you are increasingly opening up to the possibility of a serious involvement, yet on another level you hold back because you fear the loss of your freedom. Many situations feel confining now, and you in turn easily feel compromised by them.

This is the time to make constructive changes in the ways you approach the world and to strive to improve your relationship with it. Greater sensitivity and less selfishness now will add to your power. It is also important to concentrate on old unfinished emotional business that may be limiting your life potential.

The nature of the square aspect is conflict and struggle. With this particular square, when the conflict is not mastered, the end effect will be separative. Therefore, anything that you refuse to deal with now will become emotional baggage and consequently that much more complicated to master. The purpose of this life cycle is to rid yourself of all the old habits that have been holding you back from becoming a freer, greater person. Now, of course, this is not something that will happen overnight. The entire experience is a process that requires constant effort. However, the longer you ignore some of the changes you have to make, the more you will suffer, because you are holding yourself back and failing to operate from your higher self. Any pain or anxiety you feel now is for a reason. Somewhere the choices you have made for yourself have diminished your growth and freedom in that particular area.

Any self-destructive situations that you have brought upon yourself will probably end now, whether or not the change is self-imposed. The result could be very painful if you don't trust your potential to eventually attract a situation of greater possibility. Now is the time to break out of all ungenerative situations that may be eroding your *joie de vivre*. Refuse to accept limitation or you will suffer because of it.

The highest potential of this transit is to move beyond yourself to discover a greater nonpersonal reality. The challenge is to feel a larger creative and spiritual purpose to your existence. Tremendous meaning can be generated now from a serious philosophical search. Remember that all the power, joy, and love that you require is already inside of you. When you know how to bring that out of your own nature to please yourself, you will simultaneously attract the same in other people. The Uranus square tells you that nobody but you can do it and gives you the impetus to struggle through the conflict. This is the time to multiply yourself through the power of your own striving. In the end, you will find that no other struggle can promise you such an awesome reward.

Pluto Square the Sun in Leo

This is a time when your personal power is being tested, and the difficulties and conflicts that arise could be quite painful if you do not understand them. Your ego is often on the line now, and because you have such obsession with "winning," the losses experienced will hit you that much harder.

During this period there may be times when it seems that life is exploding in your face. Certain externals upon which you based much of your emotional security may go under, leaving you feeling shaken, frightened, and insecure. However, to the degree that you see your self-value only in terms of external power or material objects, you will be made more vulnerable during this period.

The keyword now is transformation. Your personal and spiritual power is being tested, forcing you to experience yourself on a higher plane. The more that you live out of your childish ego as opposed to your higher capacity of love, the more your power will be weakened by the structures that have come to control you.

A character weakness of the Leo nature is to invest too much importance in superficial status, such as money, position, title, physical appeal. While these things often do represent very positive accomplishment, they are not the only measure for self-worth. Those individuals who can not comprehend this, are ultimately controlled by them, regardless of how much corporate power they wield in the world.

If there is no safe, sane individual underneath the title, behind the bank account, beneath the flawless facade, there is no basis for a rich inner happiness, and life becomes an anxious struggle to prolong ephemeral moments that become meaningless with age. In the face of loss of status there can be only the most profound psychological devastation, since there is no inner wealth to fall back upon.

During moments of crisis now, one will be forced to confront the inner person, stripped of all exterior life props. It could be that the props will fall through or that on a deeper psychological level they no longer hold up. The entire identity is being tested now. And you are going to be forced to confront who you really are as opposed to who you would like to think you are. The external conflicts that arise in your life now will cause intense self-confrontations. If you do not really know yourself, you will be faced with pain, psychological confusion, and emotional chaos.

Leo is a sign motivated by the need to impress a very powerful self-image upon the world and to identify the self-worth with that self-image. Its archetypal challenge is to be Self- or soul-conscious. Within that higher awareness lies the greatest personal power. However, the average Leo individual is ego-conscious and consequently, whatever externals threaten the ego, also diminish the person, the entire identity, and the sense of well-being.

This is the time to discover the inspirational spark or center within yourself that is invulnerable to your material performance. This is the positive, sustaining inner self that shines regardless of negative circumstance. It is a light of hope, of possibility, of transcendence that lies already within you. Your psyche has become dimmed by your lack of conscious awareness. This is the time in your life to strive to discover that something more of yourself that will nourish you in times of crisis and enrich the entire quality of your life. In this period, the way to best solve the emotional pain is to consciously work at developing a beautiful inner self that is like a lovely home that you delight in returning to.

People often go into psychotherapy under Pluto transits because these are times of intense emotional turmoil. The problems and conflicts that are experienced now have to do specifically with a sense of powerlessness in the face of insurmountable externals.

Courage and fortitude are not enough now because on many levels of your being you are experiencing death and rebirth situations that have to be understood emotionally and spiritually. Within each situation are important lessons to be learned for the growth of a stronger, more brilliant spirit. Sweeping the rubble under the carpet will only serve the purpose of putting a Band-Aid on the wound. Eventually the Band-Aid will be ripped off by another experience, and the wound will be in worse trouble. The challenge now is to discover the profound personal meaning in the pain of each experience, meaning that will give you greater wisdom and a natural energy to go on to experience a higher quality of existence that is much brighter.

Conditions, and perhaps people, will be dying off now. You will have to face the meaning of these experiences and confront the inevitability of your own death as well. There will be moments when the facts you will have to face may seem psychologically unbearable. However, in reality what is making it seem so is the rigidity of your mind. What you have the capacity for learning now is that endings need not define you, and real success comes with the capacity to see beyond what appears to be failure or disappointment. Your fear of failure is the result of the demonic control that your ego has over you, inciting you to view life only in terms of winning and losing. When you learn to live out of your higher center, you have the ability to stand back from a painful experience instead of being dragged down underneath it. You will learn how to look at it objectively as a moment in time that does not define you and that will be followed by other moments. You will have the vision to see it as a learning experience that will ultimately make you smarter and wiser once you have managed to discover the unique meaning it has in your life.

When you develop the capacity to see all experience, both "good" and "bad," as learning experiences that offer you greater wisdom through your capacity to grow by them, the entire tenor of your life will change. You will become less anxious and far more serene. At this point the experience of living becomes richer and far more exciting because there is a sense that there is something vital to be discovered in every event. Each day you are discovering more of yourself, experiencing more on the outside, and becoming wiser and lighter on the inside. All the while, the more often you have the courage to ask yourself, "What is the unique meaning of this experience?" and "What can I learn from it to become more from it?" the more often you will come to hear the answers deep within yourself, and consequently, the more real control you will develop over your life.

For when you begin the process of unfolding your inner wisdom, you begin to awaken in yourself all the guidance in life that you will ever need. By your radiating light and self-affirmed mind, you will attract people to you who will continue to affirm you. In doing so, they will enlarge upon your capacity for higher love, and you will feel a more joyful union with all that is positive in life, including that higher aspect of your own nature.

Pluto is the planet of transformation, and as such it stimulates us to grow by making us suffer unbearably because of the negative situations that we insidiously create for ourselves. This is potentially a period of extraordinary growth, leading to great wisdom and transcendence. However, you will have to learn to relax and detach from the outside world in order to connect with the wisdom of your higher nature rising up inside you. Until you learn how to do this, try to put your problems in perspective by comparing them to situations that could be worse. It would also be helpful to read any of the number of books that I have included in my bibliography of suggested reading. Doing so will be like listening to a wise old friend who can offer you inspirational perspectives about life that you have never been able to see on your own.

If you work hard on yourself and your awareness during this period, you will eventually emerge a wise warrior, resplendent with light. It will be the light of your expanded consciousness, and it will overflow into your intelligence, your personality, your relationships, your work, and the general quality of your life.

However, before you can do that, you must first face your own darkness. You must have the courage to walk through the valley of your own shadows to seek the light. At times it may be a painful, terrifying journey. However, when you finally get there, you will have gotten beyond your own fear, and you will see everything in your life in the light of liberation, including the experience of death.

Uranus Square the Sun in Virgo

This is a cycle in your life characterized by many levels of changes that potentially could be positive but will involve some degree of emotional or psychological conflict.

On the deepest levels, what is changing now is your relationship to yourself. Part of that has to do with your self-image, and another part, with your personal goals and what you expect from your life as well as from your relationships. You have the potential now to grow up and trust yourself in new ways. Part of this will come through having more affirmative expectations, seeing your life in larger dimensions, and discovering and trusting that you can have situations that you have never allowed yourself.

The most fundamental Virgo problem is that of viewing the world in a diminishing way. Instead of enjoying a moment to the fullest, your tendency is find the fatal flaw that will create any number of problems. Often, the problems do not even exist in reality but are thought forms created by your fearful mind. You have difficulty trusting the most positive of situations, and underlying this tendency is guilt. Of all the signs, you treat yourself the least nicely. For on a bone-deep level, you never feel justified in accepting the joyful situation that you would so readily accord someone else.

There is always a nagging voice inside you hinting that you do not deserve. The degree to which you listen to that voice is the degree to which you cut off your own life force. In cutting off your life force, you are essentially cutting off your capacity to create and enjoy positive change.

There will be personal conflicts now, and because your nature is so sensitive, they will be experienced as painful. However, if you try very hard to be as self-constructive as possible, you will come away with a new, freer, more affirmative way of living inside yourself.

This is a time of personal and psychological housecleaning. The negative people who are holding you back and demanding sacrifice through their own selfish behavior must be eliminated from your life. When you do remove them, you will be shocked at the new light and vitality in your depths. This is a time to work through all external limitations. The challenge in your life now is to refuse to accept them, rather than identify with them and allow them to define you.

You have to begin to trust and love yourself now. The first step will come with learning how to say NO. Only when you can successfully say no to people, will you be able to successfully say YES to life. You must develop a center inside yourself that is based on a conscious acknowledgment of all the things you like about yourself as well as of all the expansive changes you want to enjoy creating for yourself. Virgo has a very poor sense of self. For the average Virgo, where the luminous center should be, there is instead a tight, little pocket of fear. To the degree that you allow your entire being to give in to this fear, you will stay unconscious and emotionally childish. The more childish you are, that is, the more you assign power to everything outside yourself, the more your identity will remain a darkened sun.

This is the time to rip yourself open, to take risks,

make changes, and to try to be more secure about the outcome. The more you tightly hold on to externals out of fear, the more you needlessly stagnate in your life.

The effect of Uranus in Sagittarius on your Virgo sun is that your earthbound nature feels its fire. Feel the fire in you now. Feel the anger. Feel the passion. Feel the burning excitement for all the things that you like about life. Then let that fire burn up the fear. Let its heat goad you in new directions to multiply yourself, to create possibility from each circumstance. I do not mean become an opportunist, which is essentially utilizing the best of another person for your own advantage. Use the best of yourself to master the forces on the outside. The more you master the conditions that you have passively allowed to control you, the more you will master yourself, and the more you will change and grow and brighten with the circumstance.

This is a time when you must rise to a courageous self-struggle. It is a time to say no to the limitations that are not allowing you to be a powerful individual. It is a time to test your existing powers. However, the price is that along the way you will have to sacrifice certain relationships, people, and situations that have become both comfortable and reassuring.

Such sacrifice is likely to breed fear. You may ask yourself, what if someone else does not come along? What if you never fall in love again? What if you never find a person who is so exciting and intelligent or a job situation that provides as much security? These questions will naturally arise, and in time you will find your own satisfying answers. For if you keep trying and can *really* eliminate many of your restricting fears, you will eventually find that you can control and attract ceaseless movement and endless emotional satisfaction.

Therefore, as a base step in dealing with the fear, in

order to grow into a fuller, richer, human being, try some of the following exercises. If you do these diligently, you will see results within a matter of months.

Lie down in a quiet room, close your eyes, and relax your breathing. Beginning with your feet, concentrate your consciousness on relaxing the tension in all of the muscles, moving upward to your stomach, heart center, and brain. Then slowly count backwards from thirty, and as you do, feel yourself floating away with your breathing. When you get to zero, visualize the most destructive fears that are holding you back. Anthropomorphize them and picture them as little demons. Then visualize a blazing, destructive fire that is completely out of control. Watch it eat up all of your fears, and hear the crackling. Watch each fear blacken and finally disintegrate into ashes, scattering into nothingness. Pull that fire inside your head. Feel its power and its warmth and its vitality. See yourself as the power of the fire and feel yourself rise and your magnetism increase. Then see yourself in a beautiful meadow. The sun is shining and you are at one with its warmth. You are that sun, and as you run through the tall, swaying grasses of the meadow, you feel a weightless joy like nothing you have ever felt before in your life. Now you look up at the sky, and you see your dreams flashing as if you were watching a wide-screen movie. With the power of the sun inside you, you know that you have created the movie and it is yours. You have written the script, you are the director and you always will be. Promise yourself that you will never forget this and that you will use this image to recreate possibility in the dimmer earthbound moments of living.

However, keep in mind that positive change requires time. What you will need now is time to be more positive, to rise beyond yourself and transcend yourself. However, after time has passed and you have established your radiant center, you will always have it to return to in moments of external crisis. From that center all things are possible. The brighter it grows, the greater your sense of possibility. From thereon in, life becomes an unfolding adventure.

Neptune Square the Sun in Virgo

This is a subtle period of emotional confusion, self-questioning, self-doubt, and doubt about your private world in general. Neptune is a nebulous planet and when it hits the sun sign in hard aspect, it creates a sense of nebulousness about the identity and often about goals.

The younger the person, the more difficult are the effects of this transit because of the weaker life foundations and sense of identity. The less certain the individual is of himself, of what he wants, and of the direction of his life, the more likely it is that this transit will be experienced as painful.

The pain that is experienced now comes from a feeling of personal inauthenticity in a world where everyone else appears to be happy, in love, or successfully achieving their own personal ends. Essentially, the pain issues from a weak sense of self, one that does not trust itself and is most often found in a situation of compromise.

The classic Virgo problem is—because of an inadequate self-image—the need to impose perfection on both structures and people. Everything must fall into a preestablished mode of perfection, or else it must be changed, altered, or transformed. To begin with, this restrictive attitude is difficult to deal with on a good day. However, with the influence of Neptune, all perspectives can become highly confusing and consequently your life becomes less manageable.

It is important to reexamine your standards now. Obviously, you can not change the thrust of your character and the way that you happen to think. But you can change your framework and expand your parameters. You will suffer because of your rigidity now. If you have already worked on this diminishing aspect of your personality through some form of therapy, this could be a period when you discover new life-dreams and take some risks to see where they take you.

On the other hand, if your mind is still at the mercy of your deepest doubts, this will be a time when you waver painfully. One of the primary things that you will have to deal with now is your sense of disillusion-ment. It could be that certain agreements that you have entered into precipitously will prove disappointing, both emotionally and to your entire sense of well-being. The result could be so much confusion that there is a concomitant lack of psychological energy, dullness of purpose, and inflated disillusion.

At the very worst, this could be a time when you feel almost infantile in the face of emotional needs that you have never before been conscious of. This is especially painful for you because for so much of your life you have gotten through on sheer will. However, willpow-er alone will not help you now. This is a time when what is required is a thoughtful exploration into the deeper aspects of yourself. Many Virgos live on a purely conscious, practical level, refusing to deal with the deeper emotional sides of their natures. Therefore, when their consciousness is triggered in a Neptune transit, in many ways it is as if a new person is emerging.

Neptune will have a watery effect upon your earthy psyche now. You feel more emotional than usual, and the recognition and expression of these feelings is not especially compatible with your nature. Virgo needs order, just as it needs to feel both feet on the ground and to be assured of the security that there is a ground. Now many issues in life are not as clear as you would like them to be. If you do not really know yourself, if you have spent years repressing all your painful feelings, external structures, as well as aspects of yourself, will dissolve now, and the dissolution will be disorienting. However, you must realize that this confusion and dissolution is not as meaningless as it may seen. Rather, it is the first step to change and growth, perhaps in many new directions that are more meaningful.

Without emotional development and deep psychological growth, the Virgo personality lives life mindlessly, propelled by the momentum of the routines that have come to define the life and eventually the person. During this cycle, the vibrations of Neptune are trying to soften those edges and give the personality the opportunity to see life in new ways that are more creative, open-ended, less stagnant, and more life affirming.

This is a time of questioning meanings, and questions will arise in regard to everything from career, to life purpose, to relationships, to capacity for love, to quality of love. The questions that arise now will demand answers. If you block your deeper feelings, the questions may seem unsolvable. However, if you still your mind and go into the deepest part of yourself, you may find many of the answers that your mind is seeking. If you are having a very difficult time now, it is because you are battling within yourself, and your own fear and rigidity will not allow you to go anywhere. You have to try to relax your sense of control now. Perhaps you should get a divorce, end a significant relationship, consider changing your career. Perhaps you're holding on to a structure that with time has become empty and meaningless is the reason you feel alternately chaotic and filled with the void. If you do not know yourself at all, you will have a hard time finding answers now. Many people can give you advice on your problems, however, in the end only you know what is really best for your needs. Until you develop an affirmative sense of self, you will be plagued with insecurities that diminish your self-trust every time a major, and sometimes a minor, decision must be made. The voices in your head are so conflicting that often you exist at the mercy of them, your decisions bouncing back and forth, leading you into further confusion.

Perfect emotional clarity is not something that can be established now. However, a deeper look at your own confusion can. It is important to analyze what it is specifically that you are confused about, and, more important, why you are confused. It is likely that your heart is telling you one thing and your head another. However, there is only one answer that is really right for you, and deep inside you know that to be true.

Perhaps it would be helpful to take a legal pad and mark it into three columns: decisions to be made, head's decisions, heart's desire. Fill in each column and show the list to no one. However, several times a day read each column over. If you have more confusing feelings and thoughts as you read over the list, record them in a separate notebook. Once you have your head on paper, the contents will become more orderly. What will also happen is that in the process of writing, new, liberating subconscious material will arise as well.

This is a period in which you are less realistic than usual about your life options. You are likely to overinflate the importance of certain things and to diminish others at a glance, without really giving the situation or person a try. During this cycle you are more highly fantasy-prone and have a strong tendency to be overly idealistic in your expectations. This could be a time when you consider having an extramarital affair or find yourself falling in love at first sight with a face or the force of someone's intelligence. Another possibility is that you could mentally fall in love with your fantasy of another person. However, what this person proves to be in reality could be something else altogether. As long as you try to enjoy yourself and your experiences now, without becoming bitter and sanctimonious afterward if they fail to live up to your standards, then in some way you will benefit from them.

The potential of the Neptune transit is to become acquainted with your creativity and spirituality. This is an excellent time to explore your musical talent and to take up some spiritual or philosophic study. Virgo is an introverted, studious sign, with an inherent discipline that could lead it to great self-mastery and understanding of the more esoteric aspects of life.

Consider this cycle one of exploration in which you come closer to your depths. Explore your capacity to love freely and maturely; explore your mind and heart and intellect; and in the process of the exploration, give the best of yourself while you also take the best that life has to offer you. Then, after each experience is over, drop the loss, take the gain, move on, and reflect.

Saturn Conjunct the Sun in Libra

Because Saturn is the planet of discipline and restriction, and Libra tends to be a particularly indulgent sign, this is a period that could prove to be emotionally troublesome. Saturn is a stern taskmaster, and when it transits over the sun every seven years, it demands that we begin to behave like mature adults. It forces us to take ourselves, our bodies, and our lives seriously and do the best by them. Saturn's influence is one that demands improvement and requires effort. It disapproves of our weak and self-destructive tendencies and makes us suffer because of them. Saturn's transit over the sun always brings very hard lessons, which, when learned, ultimately better life by enriching it. Whatever growth is resisted now will be paid for in the form of disappointments, depression, and divorces.

This is a time to tighten the belt, both literally and figuratively. It is a good time for dieting, all forms of self-improvement, and setting up new structures that will improve the overall quality of existence. New goals should be formulated now for every area of life. It is a time to establish more serious ideals, to make richer friendships, and to explore more substantial pastimes that will contribute to greater emotional growth.

It is possible that a love relationship will end now—if it is an emotionally compromising situation that is essentially undermining you. Any relationship that happens to end during this period is better ended. It is a time of cleaning up the life and clearing the way for richer, more life-enhancing experiences.

Saturn will challenge now any person or situation that you cling to out of fear. It will demand that you be harder on yourself, for your own good, and enjoy your life from the perspective of an adult rather than that of a spoiled child. This could very well be a time of increased responsibility and monetary pressure. It is a time in which you will find yourself working harder than usual and perhaps feeling that you are getting little accomplished. This period requires both diligence and patience. Rewards will not be immediately forthcoming. However, whatever is solid that you manage to create and establish now will in the future be something that you will be able to depend upon.

It is crucial now not to give up when disappointments dismay you. Any time you sit around and feel sorry for yourself, things are going to get worse.

This is quite often a period of diminished vitality. Therefore, it is important to take care of your health, get plenty of sleep, and be careful not to waste your energies on trivialities that in the long run add little to your life. Under this Saturn transit, it is beneficial to ask yourself what really matters, what you want most from being alive, and how you can most effectively go about getting it. However, if you merely remain at the talking stage and give in to a sense of lassitude, not only will your discontent overwhelm you, but it is also likely that your health will suffer from it as well. Sickness now will give you an excuse to escape from the onerous impingements of the outside world, since at moments what you may want most is to be taken care of. However, the better you know yourself, the more aware you will be of this destructive proclivity and thereby able to circumvent it.

Your sense of security might be something that will

be challenged now. Even if this does not happen overtly, it will become an issue that will cause you some concern. It could be that this need for security will be felt most strongly in the area of relationships. However, it could also exert its weight on your finances and career. It is important now to establish ways of taking responsibility for yourself, because you will suffer heavily from your dependencies. If you find this excessively painful, you might consider psychotherapy as an aid to developing a strong sense of self that is affirmative and sustaining. The challenge now is to develop a firm foundation within yourself, to become self-dependent, and to learn to enjoy doing it.

All periods of emptiness and loneliness now should be challenged and not indulged. Confront what is making you feel empty and lonely and take constructive measures to create the meaning you feel is lacking. This is the time to establish serious hopes and wishes and to take them beyond the talking stage.

Problems with a boss, authority figure, business partner, or coworker should not be taken personally now but should most definitely be viewed objectively. Work stress is strong now and the people around you troublesome. Life may tend to have a certain lackluster quality that seems to be wearing you thin. Apathy is not unlikely under this transit, as is also a diminished sense of self-esteem. It is this area that you have to work very hard on by reminding yourself of the love you are capable of inspiring.

Another potential problem now is fear and anxiety having to do with a deep-seated terror of loss. In the more overwhelming moments remember that all these negative feelings will eventually pass, and try to concentrate on what you want to accomplish. At all times keep in mind the potential within yourself to resolve each problem area, despite setbacks.

Most of all, do not allow your disappointments to define you, but rather view them as temporary limitations that will eventually be overcome. If you try assiduously to create some light, a path, a way for yourself, you will never lose it and it will become a part of you. Let this period be one in which you grow and learn and try and accomplish. In the end what you will gain is something beyond your dreams.

Pluto Conjunct the Sun in Libra

The challenge of this transit is self-mastery. Your sense of self is being tested now, and it is time to experience life on a deeper, more meaningful level. Slowly, old needs, fears, behavior patterns, and even relationships are dying off—to be replaced by richer, more substantial experiences. This is a time to take a creative approach to your life and to develop a new sense of self-trust, perhaps through psychotherapy.

It is important now to eliminate the habits in your life that are merely taking up your time and to replace them with new interests and friends. There may be times when you feel victimized by neurotic, self-serving friends who may seem to be taking advantage of your good will. It would be wise to first consider what originally attracted you to them. It could very well be that you unconsciously encouraged their behavior with your poor sense of self-esteem.

This is a period in which to become more conscious and self-aware. It is also a time to learn how to enjoy yourself without trying to escape from yourself through the comfort of a relationship or the company of other people. The old quality of your relationships that you previously felt grateful for is no longer satisfying. Even if you are not consciously aware of it, you are seeking positive people who have a rich sense of self that is both nurturing and sustaining. Slowly, you are becoming more aware that in order to feel the sort of excitement from life that you yearn for, you must be able to create for yourself a richer, less superficial quality of experience.

In order to create this kind of existence, it is necessary to first conquer your dependency needs. This is a time to transform your entire being, to become something more, to gain a sense of purpose that you are proud of. Therefore, it is important to reconstruct your life so that it is more meaningful and therefore more enjoyable. The first step is to stop rationalizing your limitations. The second step is to develop your will and the adult aspect of your personality, which often gives in to the child. Wishing, dreaming, and talking will not get you anywhere. Assertive action is essential now, as is your willful creation of a sense of responsibility for yourself.

This is a time of not only self-confrontation but also confrontation of your own mortality. It could be that friends or relatives or both are passing away now. This experience of loss is deeply disturbing because it brings you that much closer to your own death. It is important to deal with this fear constructively by taking up a spiritual or philosophical study or even by reading an inspiring spiritual book, perhaps on the life of a Yogi. Through this experience you will come to see both life and death in terms of possibility, not diminishment.

A classic Libra problem is your overly emotional approach to life. During this period your challenge will be to cultivate dispassion and self-restraint. It would be a good idea to step back now from personal experience and emotional frustrations and see your life with a longer view and larger perspective. Then concentrate on trusting that you will be able to create the changes you need most, even if they do not happen as quickly as you would like them to. What might prove helpful now is to write your personal goals and desires down on an index card and read them over once a day. If you are not negating them in your mind with fear or anger, in time they will materialize.

This could be a time of a rather intense, prolonged identity crisis, in which your sense of self at times seems to dissolve, leaving you lost, confused, and depressed. There may be an overwhelming sense of purposelessness, emotional disintegration, loneliness, fearfulness, and profound discontent. At some moments life may have a deadening sense of meaninglessness for you only to be followed by feelings of elation, euphoria, ecstacy. These positive feelings are glimpses of greater possibility forcing their way out from your subconscious mind.

The black periods are experiences of the old, dark unaware consciousness dying off. They are a signal that there is more of you to be explored than you are using. They are telling you that what you have chosen so far for yourself is limiting your very sensibilities. All feelings of self-hatred now are indications that a new self is painfully struggling to be born. However, the only way that that new, stronger self can emerge is through "labor." The more you passively refuse to participate in your own self-birth, the greater will be the pain. You bring about your pain through your resistance and through your own reluctance to work toward greater emotional growth. Childish self-indulgence now will ultimately lead to an emotional demise if you use your pleasure-seeking ways as escapes. Stuffing food down your mouth may suppress the pain for a while. However, ultimately you will have to face yourself— and any subsequent self-destructive fat. All excess now will eventually leave you feeling apathetic. This is the time to test your unique power by learning the value of discipline and striving. It is a time to establish new, expansive goals, and to concentrate on new areas of knowledge. In addition, you must focus your attention in a disciplined fashion on achieving what you have set before you. The challenge now is to take command of yourself and your life and to make the entire experience an exciting adventure into hitherto unknown regions.

If any conditions end in your life now, it is ultimately for a constructive purpose—even if you don't realize it at the first. These are the people or situations that are holding you back from becoming more. This is your opportunity to enrich your inner reaches so that your life will expand with possibility. It is up to you alone to create it—never settle for less *from yourself*.

It is possible now to meet a "fated" love or a person who has become manifest through your subconscious desires. Anyone with whom you become intensely involved now is providing an experience that your consciousness needs for greater growth. This situation will not necessarily be your ideal love. In fact, it could be someone who is magnetic, yet selfish and powerful, who demands that you give up too much of yourself for the sake of the romance, thereby giving you the opportunity to win the challenge of standing up for yourself. On the other hand, it could also be someone highly evolved and with whom you are forced to compromise some of your superficial values in order to continue the relationship. Whoever you attract will be on the level that your consciousness is operating from. Somewhere within the power of that attraction is a liberating lesson that must be learned.

Saturn Conjunct the Sun in Scorpio

The primary challenge during this life cycle, which will last a little over two years, will be to confront and eliminate your fears. This is a difficult transit, for Saturn in the sign of Scorpio has a much heavier vibration than in the previous sign, Libra.

Scorpio is the sign of death and regeneration. It is the deepest, most complex sign in the zodiac, so complex that many Scorpio individuals know little of themselves—many of their fears and motivations remain unconscious throughout their life. Scorpio is a dark sign that must work to free itself of its psychological bandages to reach the light. The average Scorpio individual is a smart, shrewd, deeply feeling, and very complicated individual who often lives emotionally like someone wearing an overcoat in the middle of August. There is often an unexpressed seriousness to the nature that is so profound that it is not dealt with consciously. At the root of that seriousness is a terror of aloneness that is so deeply rooted in the psyche that the average Scorpio individual usually compensates for it by sublimating it into a powerful career drive, which is in reality a drive for a sense of personal power. The Scorpio individuals who are not driven to strive are the ones who carry a tremendous rage that they have turned against themselves. They will express it through passive, clinging, dependent, and sometimes masochistic behavior, which is seen more often in the women of this sign. The power-driven men and the women who have masculinized their drives into intense, compulsive, material striving are partially affirming their identity and partially anesthetizing themselves to their anxiety about aloneness.

Scorpio is a highly repressive sign that habitually blocks its deeper conflicts and throws its more disturbing feelings toward the back of the brain. Intense, emotional sexual relationships are usually painful and are often avoided in favor of superficial ones because they arouse an anxiety and terror of abandonment that for many Scorpio minds is deathlike. Unconsciously, what the average Scorpio mind creates as a life-style is an emotionally sublimative career and a comfortable, cozy, monotonous marriage that poses no challenge, but also offers no threat.

During this transit all "coziness" will be challenged as Saturn in your sign will force tightly repressed fears to crawl out of the woodwork. The degree to which they're tucked back is the degree to which you will experience depression under this transit.

This is a time of heavy moodiness, not actually caused by the planet Saturn, but catalyzed as its energies stimulate the depths of your unconscious fears. Life around you will become a Rorschach of your defense mechanisms now, and you will have to face yourself and start to get to know that person on the inside.

The empty relationships you cling to now out of fear will make you lonely, despondent, and miserable, and the most natural escape will be in your dedication to your work. However, under this transit it will be difficult to experience the same feeling of gratification. Disappointments may arise, hassles and unforeseen difficulties. The pressures of the material world will at times make you feel diminished, empty, and inhuman. The spark of life will dull, and you will wonder how it was ever there.

Marriages and relationships often break up under Saturn. However, it will be more characteristic of your nature to cling to the comfort of whatever security you happen to have at hand. Health problems can arise now, as your vitality and energy will be at an all time low.

Any relief to be found during the low points of this period will be governed by the quality of your personal relationships, your willingness to explore and enrich your inner reaches, and the degree of your personal desire for growth. Blind repression will bring you everything from pain in the depths of your soul to sickness. You must confront yourself now, grow within yourself, and try to get beyond yourself into a new, wiser, brighter person. There is tremendous wisdom to be called upon in the Scorpio consciousness. Your challenge during this cycle is to tap it and to transform yourself into a more fully conscious being who has real control over suffering.

First you must confront your deepest fears and come to fully understand the degree of their irrationality. However, you must travel through your fears in order to be freed by them. Saturn is the planet associated with fear. One of the painful aspects of this period is that you will feel more profoundly fearful about many different aspects of yourself. However, on some level, a kernel of truth will be trying to free itself in your consciousness and that truth is your state of ultimate aloneness. Within the Scorpio psyche is the awareness that we are ultimately all alone and that all security in between is ephemeral and illusory. This truth may be viewed in a negative way now, and your irrational fears will make you unconsciously sense this as self-diminishment.

However, when you go within yourself to discover more of yourself, to discover your higher, wiser spirit, and form a union with it, you will come to see your aloneness as something positive, joyful, and interconnecting, in the most profound, meaningful way, with other people and forces in the universe.

The degree to which you are living a shallow, unconscious life will be the degree of your pain now. The important lesson to be learned is that your emotional state reflects the quality of life that you have chosen for yourself. If your relationships and inner life are like stagnant pools, then your mind will feel like a stagnant pool now. However, if you have gotten beyond your ego and are able to be seriously and responsibly in love, then the richness of that love will generate its own life force in the midst of any darkness around you.

Yet love for another is still not enough. For during this period you must learn how to love yourself as well. Before you can do that, you have to begin to really know yourself as opposed to existing mechanically within yourself.

A first necessary step in this exploration is therapy. Along with that, you must try to establish new relationships and pastimes that not only enrich your nature but also call upon the highest, wisest part of yourself. Your spirit must be uncovered now, brought out from under all the years of being cloaked in role playing. You must also learn to look at your life from a less rigid and more open-ended perspective.

It is important to fully understand now that you do not have to be depressed or apathetic during this period. The depression is not caused by the planet Saturn but by the profound, complicated resistances within your psyche that are blocking your psychological drive to create more affirmative conditions. The most profound and at the same time the most practical truth underlying occult doctrine is that we create our own reality from our thoughts and beliefs. The conditions of our life, even the state of our physical appeal is the result of our thought forms. It is possible to change not only the conditions of our life but also our physical attractiveness through the use of our mind.

However, the problem is that most people are not even aware of the contents of their mind. They are not conscious of the fears and anger and negative thinking that are repressed and operate powerfully on an unconscious level. It will do no good to tell yourself daily that you are beautiful or that you can attract love if there is still a rigid unconscious conviction to the contrary.

Therefore, before significant constructive change can occur, it is necessary to know the deeper contents of your mind and the beliefs and ideas that are preventing the fulfillment of positive desires. So if you feel depressed now, it is for concrete reasons unique to your particular psyche. The following exercise could be very helpful: In a very quiet room sit by yourself and contemplate your feelings. Take a pad and pencil and write them down. In a separate column, write down the beliefs that seem to be supporting them. Then in a third column, see if you can pull out the fears that are supporting these beliefs. Things could come up out of your unconscious now that may truly surprise you. If you are successful at this exercise, and it may take a while to free your mind enough to be successful, then what you will ultimately realize, looking at your separate columns, is that underlying every emotional or material disappointment is a fear.

Examine those fears. Do not push them back into unconscious awareness and do not let them intimidate you. Look at the fear from all perspectives. First of all, see it as one choice you have for looking at your life. But see it as a choice you have made during the past and not necessarily one you will make in the future. Then make a list of other beliefs that could be substituted for the fear.

Again, in two separate columns, record the fear in column one and in column two record as many other perspectives as you can think of from which to view that aspect of yourself in a more positive, as well as a realistic, way. If you can see the fear as one of many choices that you can make about your own life, you will begin to feel much freer.

Underlying all the individual fears is the fear of *trusting yourself* to bring into your life the conditions you most want. If you are depressed now, it is because you are reinforcing this self-distrust in a variety of mental and emotional ways.

One way may be by comparing yourself to others you feel have greater fortune, power, fame, or love. However, regardless of what you may want to believe, there is really no such thing as luck. Anyone who has more than you, does so because he likes himself more, to the extent that he trusted that he deserved whatever it was that he desired. Life is that simple. If on the deepest levels, you feel that you are unworthy of your desires, that you do not really deserve what you want most, then your life will most definitively be fraught with emotional conflict, difficulty, and disappointment.

The only way to change your life, your career, the promise of your future is to change yourself. All Scorpios deeply believe that everything in their life is deeply complicated. However, the complications that exist for them come about only because of their tendency to view life that way. Try now to see your life more simplistically. Begin with one simple premise—your own *unique* power.

Decide what sterling attributes you have that make you appreciated by those who know you, and list them on a piece of paper. Humor, wisdom, profound emotional understanding—begin with the qualities that you most enjoy in yourself. Also include on the list your accomplishments, all the positive aspirations that you have fulfilled in your life that you are proud of and want to define you. Take time now to contemplate the power that your unconscious mind knows to be in you and try to identify with that feeling of power.

See all disappointments now as passing moments on an endless continuum. Do not hold on to the disappointments and allow them to color the tone of your life or your future. Instead, make a game plan of the experiences that you do want to color your future, that you want to define you as a uniquely powerful individual. When you really connect to that power that is already within you, you will live your life from a place of such self-affirmation that you will actually increase your electromagnetic force-field to influence all those around you. That does not mean that you will be able to change the pesonality of your problematic boss or colleague. But it does mean that eventually your self-affirmative beliefs will create more positive conditions— either within or without the job structure. And this goes for every aspect of your life—from love to career goals.

In the area of love, the most profound Scorpionic fear is the twin fear of death and abandonment. There is always the anxiety that a wonderful moment or exciting love may never come again. However, that is merely a *belief* incurred by the fearful tendencies of your consciousness. If you have seen that happen in your life, it is because you have *believed* that it would happen.

Your fears have materialized into reality. However, had you been able to expect something different from life, a different reality would have manifested.

What you should learn during this seven-year cycle is that you will always pay a heavy emotional price for the fears that you continue to hold on to. You do not have to hold on to them. Nor do you need to suffer. First, however, instead of concentrating on your fear of endings, focus on expanding yourself and your positive emotional awareness, as you develop your entire potential daily. If you concentrate your energies on seeing each life experience as a potential from which something positive can be gained, then you will be slowly reorienting your thinking process to eliminate fear rather than repress it. See all losses as opportunities for something better to come along, and stand back from your pain in eager anticipation of the next positive experience. If you concentrate on self-knowledge, self development, self-expansion, and self-love, you will ultimately find all the answers, power, light, and beauty inside of yourself to create the life you want. Work very hard to trust that you can have it. The changes that you will ultimately enjoy will be nothing less than the miracles of your own mind.

Uranus Conjunct the Sun in Scorpio

This is a long period of change, the challenge of which is to become freed from your fears in order to become more in your life. It is a time of many expected and unexpected endings and beginnings. On the surface, the life changes could involve new jobs, relationships, marriages, divorces, career changes, or even new children. However, whatever the specific change happens to be, you must realize that something in you needed it.

Although everything that you are undergoing now will ultimately be affirmative, there could be a painful severance aspect, exacerbated by your deep-seated need for security. However, this is the time to begin to learn how to let go of what you do not need. Like a surgeon with a scalpel, it is necessary to try to cut yourself free of the compulsions, obsessions, and fears that are diminishing your enjoyment of life. Psychotherapy could be extremely beneficial now in helping you to become more conscious of your self-restrictive behavior patterns.

Ideally, this could be the time to discover new freedom, to probe your own creativity, and to explore new experiences that will expand your heart, soul, and mind. Aspire now to spontaneous experience in all areas of your life, especially love and friendship. This is a time to love in a freer manner, divorced from fear and deep-seated abandonment anxiety. It is a period in which you must strive to move beyond your psychological harnesses and learn to enjoy your life with greater inner freedom. In order to do this you must learn how to relax and take experience and especially yourself less seriously. Your deep-seated need to possess could be undermining your sense of well-being now. Likewise, you need to strive for greater objectivity in all of your undertakings and interactions. It could be that a close relationship is not giving you all the feeling or passion that you feel you need. Perhaps it would be best to stop, step back, and evaluate the situation in a larger perspective. Maybe through your own compulsions you are distorting the situation and consequently constricting the other person's freedom.

Any situation that you are clinging to now out of fear alone is likely to break apart, forcing you to confront the deepest aspects of yourself. Stagnant emotional situations may produce an underlying discontent now. This is the time to ride with change. Even if at moments you feel that your life is getting crazy and that perhaps a part of you is disintegrating, go with it, and try to trust that it is a transformative experience and not the end. See all changes now as exciting opportunities for new experience where you have the potential to enjoy your life to a much greater degree.

Ideally, life can be an adventure now. Absolutely anything can happen if you can get in control of your fears. If it is a relationship that has ended, concentrate less on the feeling of loss, and instead consider objectively all of the ways it failed to fulfill you. Spend some time formulating a list of ideal qualities that you would like to find in someone new. Then write them down and read them to yourself every day.

Making lists of all kinds is a constructive way to sort out your feelings and make your life feel more manageable. Devote one column to what you dislike or disturbs you, and underneath it make a list of solutions or alternatives that might be preferable or at least fun to try. Make a game out of it and challenge yourself to think up as many different choices as you can. When you have a problem set down on paper, it will lose some of its awesomeness as you gain a sense of possibility.

It might seem now that you feel split in two and conflicted at the deepest levels of your being. Perhaps you feel caught between what you feel you need and what you want ideally. These tensions can manifest through your body, making you unusually high-strung, irritable, and unable to sleep. Strenuous physical activity is a good way to relieve surface tension. However, remember that this tension is merely a symptom of something deeper that has to be dealt with. Jogging your life away isn't going to reconstruct a disintegrating life situation, although it may help you to think more clearly and ultimately to deal with the problem. The point is that until you confront your deeper intense feelings, the tenor of your life will remain a tense repetitive pattern.

Try not to think in terms of loss now. Instead, make an effort to turn every situation into one of possibility. Train your mind to change things to your advantage even if something appears negative at the onset. If you cannot find a way to alter the situation immediately, then try to find a way to change your attitude. Try to trust in the inevitability of more positive change. Uranus in your sign is heralding profound psychological changes that will challenge many of the old, stagnant situations you have come to take for granted. Now is the time to begin to live your life like a sage who trusts his power to take from life what he affirmatively desires. In order to get to this point, it is necessary for you to deal with your repressed and suppressed anger, which tends to control you from within. When this is not expressed constructively, you live in its clutches, subject to its strokes through attacks of moodiness, anxiety, and depression.

During this period you must reevaluate your entire life and see it through the framework of greater possibility and inner freedom. For those who are able to master this challenge, it can be a most exciting time, characterized by new friendships, interests, and attitudes about the self, life, and love. From this new perspective all things are possible, everything can lead to something better, and there is no loss, only change. This is a time of heightened intuition, originality, insight, and, ideally, inspired creation. Sudden insights, flashes, and opportunities await you now, and all you have to do is relax your mind to receive them. All the power that you'll ever need is already deep inside you. This is the time to discover it and find out where it can take you.

Pluto Conjunct the Sun in Scorpio

The transit of Pluto in the sign of Scorpio is a very slow transit of many years and will have a profound personal as well as generational effect. This is a time of slow, transformative change.

On a mass level, this transit heralds biological and nuclear world events that will have a consummate effect upon the way that people live their lives. Potentially, it is a time of an evolutionary world-consciousness, characterized by concern and caring about the quality of existence, and instigated by political and environmental problems.

On an individual level, it is a time of psychological crisis, change, death, and rebirth. It is a breaking up of conditions, revealing a potential of heightened awareness and deeper self-realization.

There will be endings, but there will also be important new beginnings now. Stagnant conditions will come to an end, making room for richer, more vital sorts of experience.

The Pluto cycle is the most serious cycle of becoming. Potentially, it is a period of self-mastery, through striving on new emotional levels, and of creating a life that is richer in meaning. A new self is being born now, and as it emerges there will be labor pains in the form of moodiness, emotional confusion, depression, and feelings of alienation. These moments are opportunities to recognize a positive part of yourself that you have been unconsciously holding back.

Scorpio is the most complicated sign in the zodiac. It is highly intuitive yet also unconscious of many of its moods and motivations. Whenever there is a low mood-swing in this sign, it is a signal that there is repressed material that is leaking through the conscious awareness and straining to come out. Quite often these emotions are feelings of anger that have gone unexpressed for a very long time. However, sometimes they are also profound, deep-seated fears of death, disappointment, abandonment, and loneliness. These feelings are the distortions of a complicated mind at war with its contents. The more that these fears are brought up into the conscious mind, to be dealt with and dismissed, the more the inner person will be freed and the greater the sense of well-being.

Control is a key aspect of the Scorpionic personality, and it will be your controls that will be tested now. The areas involved could be the dying off of a relationship, a job, a career, or a person, affecting the way you look at your life. These experiences are opportunities for finding a wiser self and a freer way of functioning. However, to the degree that your personality is rigid, fearful, and inflexible, you will also experience pain.

This cycle is a challenge to transform your inner center by relying on the highest aspects of your nature, which are self-love, self-trust, and compassion for your fellow man. The more that you learn to free yourself from your inner reaches and to experience the loftiness of your own nature, the greater will be your power and your potential for new joy.

Self-mastery is the key word now. One of the prime areas in which this will be tested is your capacity to love freely. Although Scorpio is the most deeply emotional sign, often what passes for love in a Scorpio native is really a number of other things. Manipulation, security, and mind games are often the negative means that you employ to gain and maintain what you feel to be the necessary control in your life. However, what you usually do not see is the degree to which these controls control you. There may be many times when these techniques backfire on you, and emotionally you may feel as if someone has slammed a door in your face. During such moments the only thing to do is to surrender to the feeling and pass through it. Then, as the pain passes away, ask yourself what you can possibly learn from it.

Answers will come, and they will free you from the inside. Eventually, many answers will give you that much more strength and wisdom to call upon during difficult conditions.

You may face many of your worst fears now. Through facing them you will have the opportunity to master them and move beyond them—forever. However, you will have to watch your thoughts on a daily basis and not repress your emotional response when it starts to rise within you.

Your entire identity is being tested now, and at times you may feel confused about who you are and what you really want. At times you may feel terrified of change altogether because on a very deep level you associate it with loss. However, the trick is to see yourself as a person who is continually growing beyond yourself. Measure that growth by developing the habit of looking back upon your life to see how far you have come. Regardless of your fears, see your life as a process of becoming in which there are no stopping points. Try to make even the negative experiences work for you by making self-knowledge, self-love, and self-trust the conscious goal for each outcome. If you live this way, eventually an elevating wisdom will arise within you that will bring you beyond yourself. Your mind, your heart, your entire being, will be transformed.

Neptune Conjunct the Sun in Sagittarius

The tone of this transit is more psychological than event-oriented. Neptune brings on moods. It clouds the clarity of the consciousness and instills mental and emotional confusion. Therefore, this might be a time when you feel more disorganized, not only about your responsibilities, but also about yourself, your self-image and sense of purpose in life. It is impossible to predict precisely what this transit will bring about. However, on the negative side, this confusion can range from self-delusion to depression. There is often an aching dissatisfaction with existing life circumstances and a feeling of powerlessness about being able to change them. Situations and old relationships may dissolve peculiarly, and infections and psychosomatic disorders may temporarily impair normal functioning. In general, this could be a period of peculiar misunderstandings and dissolving situations, arising from self-delusions, self-doubt, and self-recriminations.

Fantasies often run strong now. Certain fantasy situations materialize at the same time that other stable situations disintegrate. This is a period in which you are more prone to feel victimized. That does not mean that, in actuality, you are. It is very difficult to be objective now. Therefore, it is a time when you may feel highly irrational and unable to maintain emotional control.

On an underlying level there is a need for some sort of release from the constrictions of life's limitations.

Certain routines that were previously unquestioned may now become deadening. However, depending on the level of awareness, this sensation may remain largely subliminal.

This discontented feeling that nothing is enough may instigate a wide range of behavior and emotional states. At the very worst, there may be self-destructive tendencies, the cause of which is a sense of apathy and alienation. At times, living may be like viewing others through a thick plate-glass window and feeling a sense of hopelessness about being able to connect. Your concentration may also be poor, and therefore it might be more difficult now to become or remain focused. There may be a strong desire to escape through drugs or alcohol. In addition, there could be extremely dangerous reactions to drugs.

However, I wish to emphasize that this experience is the worst experience of Neptune. Not everyone will feel this way, and the determining factor is the individual level of emotional awareness and spiritual evolvement. This period is potentially the most difficult when there is no spiritual or creative meaning in the life. It is my strong opinion that the most constructive way to deal with this transit is through artistic expression or spiritual exploration.

This is an important time to explore all of the creative possibilities within your unique consciousness and to try to touch upon inspirational resources that you've never tapped. Take piano lessons or a course in abstract painting, or buy yourself some brushes and play with tempera. Go to a lecture on some spiritual subject. Take a course in the Tarot. Investigate a guru center. Read the *Autobiography of a Yogi* by Paramahansa Yogananda. Then look in the mirror and say daily, "All the power that I'll ever need is here right now."

A general tendency now is to feel glamorized by

experience or to seek to feel glamorized. This is a time when you are searching for heroes, gurus, and the grand love. They may all appear, only to ultimately disappear. In addition, what your expansive expectations insist is a messiah of possibility, could in reality be unmasked as a villain. Therefore, it is important to allow yourself enough room for growing and learning but at the same time to cushion yourself in case the bottom should disappear quite suddenly. Now is not the best time to give away your family fortune or risk it at Las Vegas, or speculate your savings on the stock market. This is a time when grand loves and great schemes may be constructed far more from far-blown fantasies and wishful thinking than from a realistic basis.

Neptune has a lot to say on the subject of security. In the first place, it tells us that it is pure illusion. In the second place, an illusion that we do not really need. Neptune rules drugs, and its effect on the brain is a druglike effect on the life. Hallucinogenic insights that involve reality testing are an essential Neptunian statement. The Neptunian message is that we are all boundless and profoundly interrelated. Separateness is as much illusion as the structures that appear to be dissolving. Solitariness is no more than a thought pattern that diminishes the possibility of ceaseless possibility.

Neptune is the higher octave of the love experience. It is the selfless love that issues from the highest aspect of the soul. Neptune is the love that is neither based on security needs nor entertainment. Rather, it is the transcendent experience of wanting only the greatest joy for another person.

However, this self-sacrificing ideal is not always ideal in everyday life. If you offer yourself to someone unworthy, it will result in eventual loss. This is why Neptune is such a difficult planet. It incites us to rise to an ideal and dissolve our human fears to embrace it regardless of the cost. Its energies blind us with the glory of a moment. Its mystical statement is that that is all that we really have.

This premise is incongruent with human postures based on attachment, fear, and psychological defense. Therefore, the more earthbound we are, the more difficult it is to deal with Neptune's nebulous vibrations. Neptune is the planet of universal love, mystical contemplation, and musical genius. It is easiest to deal with its vibration in a Buddhist monastery or meditating on a mountain top. However, in a business suit or on a busy highway, the best one can do is keep to the road.

On the level of a routinized rat-race existence Neptune is moodiness, the glory of fantasy, and the need to escape. Divine highs are sought now from all sides of the spectrum. The most constructive way to obtain these highs is from a transcendent creative or spiritual experience.

Like the other slow-moving planets, Neptune is an expander of consciousness. The people who are not interested in growing emotionally, spiritually, or creatively are going to have a confusing time. The possibilities that Neptune offers to the average person are neither easy to see nor grasp logically. That's because it is trying to make us aspire to become more than average. Through the vibrations of Neptune we are taken somewhere in time, and whether the direction is "heaven" or "hell" depends on the flow and growth of our own minds and how open we are to exploring our own potential.

Uranus Conjunct Sun in Sagittarius

This could be a most exciting time, for the tenor of this transit is change, something that comes easily to your restless Sagittarian personality. However, if you have been living in a disorganized fashion, this transit may make you more erratic, restless, and irresponsible than usual. Now is the time when you may feel an overwhelming desire to make each moment the most exciting. This type of restless adventure-seeking can ultimately leave you bored and jaded if your quest is merely confined to the surface of life.

However, if you are more interested in spiritual growth, this could be a rich time that is vital and generative. It is a time to discard what you do not need while you discover new aspects of yourself that take you beyond yourself.

You may feel more nervous now, more excitable, and more in need of freedom. Confining situations will have a constraining effect upon your nervous system, perhaps leaving you craving all kinds of escapes. At moments you may feel irritable, high-strung, and ready to explode. Situations may fall apart or test your patience. Temporarily, instantaneous irritations or altercations may leave you feeling chaotic and out of control. At a certain point, you may also feel the necessity of weeding out your life to form fewer, more substantial friendships.

All kinds of change are imminent now. It is up to you to make this period as vital as possible. Mental, emotional, and psychological changes will arise that will push you to new horizons and experiences. However, at times life may also seem so chaotic that it might feel impossible to get everything accomplished that you need to get accomplished. However, at the same time, it is important to try to flow with what may seem to be the craziness and not allow it to diminish your life in any way.

The most positive aspect of this period has to do with the expansion of self into higher, more exciting spiritual dimensions. This is a time when anything can happen, and often situations seem to materialize like a bolt from the blue. This is an excellent time in which to meet new people and to develop more stimulating friendships. You will be experiencing deep psychological change now, and you will gradually be looking at your life differently and may even come to see the experience of loving in a different way.

The challenge is to get beyond your ego now, to care and experience love in a much less selfish way. That does not mean that you should be self-sacrificing but, rather, caring from the highest aspects of yourself, —responding to the beauty of another person's inner reaches instead of being concerned with what you are going to get. This freer kind of love, which is beyond anxiety, will bring you greater happiness and a more free-floating feeling of joy. Ideally, your response to many different kinds of people will be on this higher level, and you may find now that it is possible to love many different people in many different kinds of ways.

This could be a highly idealistic time in which you formulate new ideals and work to make your dreams come true. Spiritual and philosophical interests could bring your life great meaning now, and this should be something that you pursue quite seriously. With the vibration of Uranus affecting your psyche, this is the time when it would be very easy to intuit many liberating truths. However, you must first educate your mind through reading systems of elevating thought.

Situations that end now are situations that are arresting your growth. Ideally, you should work within the frameworks of your existing relationships to eliminate stagnancy and promote generative climates characterized by positive change. During this period, you will become increasingly aware of time and anxious that you have something positive and concrete to show for it. The challenge is to move beyond yourself and feel more, care more, and become more, and finally to let that state of becoming define you.

This is a time to take your life into your hands and move toward the stars. There are no limits to the possibilities that lie before you. The only restriction is your own imagination. Let it bring you along on a never-ending journey of greater and greater joy.

Saturn Square the Sun in Capricorn

This is a time of self-struggle and development, the challenge of which is to grow beyond the rigidity of your fears and defenses. There may be disappointments and setbacks now that should be carefully evaluated. Each one is a door, an opportunity to know yourself better and to grow from that awareness.

It is a tendency of the Capricorn nature to be too critical and too self-critical. You will suffer now from your propensity to diminish experience. At times you may feel a profound dissatisfaction with your life. Confront these feelings and force yourself to decide what it is that you are doing or not doing to contribute to them.

This is a period in which you may feel overly concerned with your self-image. On one day you may feel that you have the sort of power that you desire. However, on the next you may feel depressed, and obsessed with the limitations of yourself or your life. Your ego is being tested now, and the challenge of this period is to move beyond it to live a freer, richer life. However, before you are truly able, it is first necessary to descend into your darkness to sort out some shadowy aspects of your consciousness. To the degree that you refuse to do this, your emotional and physical health may also suffer. Psychosomatic problems are common now, depending on the level of your total awareness.

The external props and values that you have created

for yourself may feel incomplete now. In fact, life itself may feel incomplete, leaden, and lacking. Hopefully, this will spur you on a quest for new values and experiences that will give your life a richer, inner meaning. It is only through the path of self-discovery that you will find the kind of psychological freedom that is deeply sustaining. If you are in pain, this is a sign that there is something wrong with the way you are living. Somewhere you have chosen a pattern that is restricting your potential for inner peace and happiness. It is likely that you have settled into this state because of your deep-seated fears of inferiority.

There is no amount of power that will give the Capricorn nature enough ego-reassurance. Deep inside there are always doubts that are usually catalyzed through social or emotional situations. Often you have problems loving because you bring so much of your ego to the experience. It is very difficult for you just to let go and be at one with the positiveness of the feeling. Instead, you are always standing back, wondering what you look like and worrying. Until you learn to relax the rigid, critical hold you have over your emotions, you will always be at war with yourself, creating obstacles to what you really want. Deep inside you feel a sense of inadequacy, which you project on the outside world. Too often you expect to be let down and therefore create an elaborate set of defenses to arm yourself against this happening. This is the time to become aware of how these defenses undermine you and to stand back from them.

During this Saturn cycle, many of these feelings will be brought to the surface, and the areas in which they will be played out will be in both business and personal relationships. Relationships may end now because of the changes going on within you. It is important to thoughtfully evaluate each experience and consider how you can learn from it something psychologically liberating about yourself.

Psychotherapy would be highly advisable now. However, you can also grow from standing back from yourself and developing a sense of humor about yourself. This will take time, persistence, and constant effort. However, the freedom from self-bondage that potentially can be achieved is more than worthwhile.

Conflicts experienced now with other people offer important opportunities to look at yourself, your life, and the quality of your relationships in a more trenchant manner. If things are not working to your satisfaction, you must ask yourself why and formulate a more profound, sensitive awareness. You must also reflect thoughtfully upon ways that you can transform your own behavior to attract a better quality of experience.

It is essential that you grow from within now and expand your consciousness and your way of looking at the world. Eventually you must realize that it is the limitations that you impose upon yourself and others that restrict your life, love, and capacity to feel freely. Life can be whatever you want it to be. However, first you have to work on the fears deep inside yourself that are not allowing it to happen.

Use your frustrations and conflicts now as learning experiences that you grow from. It is important that you understand that the difficult moments are necessary even if they are painful, for when you master them, you master yourself and move beyond yourself. Ideally, life should be a continual becoming in which we increasingly free ourselves to enjoy more of ourselves. However, to explore yourself successfully, it is also necessary to stand back from yourself and your relationships to see the dynamics objectively. The more selfish you are, the more self-conscious and the more miserable you will be. On the other hand, the richer your inner being is, the more lofty will be your capacity for feeling and the greater will be your potential for joy. The more that you can get beyond yourself to feel and care for other people, the more expansive will be your life and the happier you will become. In the Capricorn nature, the road is all or nothing. Either you operate from the strictures of your Saturnian nature and thereby keep yourself in bondage, or you operate from your higher self and become a vehicle of love and its possibility. The lessons of Saturn now will give you the opportunity to move toward that potential. If you remain spoiled, petulant, and infantile, you are going to pay the price for it repeatedly.

Now is the time to work toward a higher quality of being. It will take work, most definitely. However, as you begin to see the liberating changes in yourself you will be the first to announce how much the work was worth it.

Pluto Square the Sun in Capricorn

This is a serious time of transformation and emotional growth, often sparked by relationship difficulties and sometimes health problems, which will differ in severity. Your sense of security may be challenged now as old situations that you had come to trust are dying off. The death and rebirth aspect of Pluto is very often a painful one. It is painful primarily because there are profound emotional changes in yourself that you do not want to face.

A deep-seated Capricorn problem is insecurity. Although your facade is strong, cool, and controlling, often you suffer intense self-doubt underneath. While, on the surface, people see you as strong, and perhaps overpowering, underneath you never completely trust yourself and therefore erect strong ego-defenses to protect yourself. When these defenses begin to control your personality, they also begin to control your relationships and the quality of them. That defensive part of your personality must be transformed now. The people problems that occur will come about because of your resistance to your own emotional growth.

What you should strive for now is balance—between the inner and the outer you, between your ability to take and to give. Whatever is out of balance will cause you painful problems now. The effects may appear to be coming from the outside, but they are really a part of your frustrated consciousness, seeking to free itself in a deeper experience of life.

The deepest part of you needs to be free to love more fully now. Yet, you cannot love if you are deeply locked within the bonds of your defensive behavior. You can only love freely if you first come to love and trust yourself. Otherwise, you will continue to unconsciously project your fears onto situations and people, ultimately bringing about the rejection and disappointment that you fear so deeply.

This is a time in which you have to learn to think positively on all levels of your being. You have to learn to enjoy yourself and to try to trust that what you want to come to you will come—even if not as quickly as you would like. The problems and difficulties that you will be experiencing now are your gateways to possibility. At the most difficult times, try to stand back from your ego and seriously consider the feelings of others, as you reflect on what you might learn about yourself from the conflict in the situation.

Some of the frustrations that plague your life now will leave you feeling that you have a frightening lack of control. This will be particularly distressing because of your need to assert control in most situations. The challenge of this period is to realize that even though things may temporarily fall through for you, it is not the end of the world; there is a tomorrow that will bring something better. You have to affirm this potential in spite of outward conditions. It is your ability to hope and trust that is being tested now, and there will be moments when you may feel that the fear will not allow you. However, if you persist in holding fast to your positive vision, you will eventually create the doors and opportunities that you desire. The greatest difficulty of this period is that, although frustrations may come from the outside, you will be waging complicated battles within yourself simultaneously. At times you may feel that you are undergoing such profound psychological change that you are dying and being reborn on many different levels of your being. You must trust that each ending also holds its own beginning—even if you can't see what it is at the time.

Perhaps the most difficult aspect of this period is that it may promote a painful identity crisis. If you are unsure of who or what you are, where you are really going in life, what it is you really want, these conflicts will come to the surface, causing you to suffer much confusion. At the same time, it is likely that you will feel simultaneously a need for greater power, a desire to assert yourself, and a need to enlarge your worth through accomplishment, all to a greater degree than you have ever felt in your life before.

The essential pain of this period is that you want more than you have ever wanted and more than you feel you deserve. Yet, frustratingly so, the wheels keep getting stuck, perhaps the spokes fall apart and a gargantuan amount of energy is required to keep everything running.

There are important decisions you must make now and new aspects of your life that you have to create as well. There may be times when you feel not only impatient but fairly frantic about getting on with the entire process. Things are not the way you want them to be, and at moments you suffer deeply and silently about what you feel to be your unique dissatisfactions. You will have a strong tendency now to identify your self-image with your capacity to create positive change. This can be very dangerous because when you feel profoundly thwarted, you will feel that your own personal power is diminished. This is a natural response, especially if there is no one around you to reinforce your positive self-image. When you begin to doubt yourself and your ability to create from life what you want most, the resulting negation of self could create a profound depression.

There may be times during this period when, despite all effort, you simply feel rotten, lonely, and fearful of the future. It is very important that you do not hold these feelings inside of you, as will be your propensity. What you need now are new perspectives on your life, which can be gained, not only from a wise psychotherapist, but also from intelligent, loving, trusted friends. The rigidity in your nature will not make it easy for you to confide or communicate the depths of your pain. Because of this, you will probably try to force yourself away from your feelings and into increasingly frenzied activity in an effort to free yourself of the vulnerability you feel. Yet, despite your schemes and routines, the pain will return in the form of fluctuating mood-swings that can be severely disorienting. The more you run away from yourself, the more you seek oblivion from your feelings, the more you reach for meaning merely in the material, the more powerful will be the force of your feelings when they return.

The only deep inner relief that you will find now will be through your capacity to love yourself and others. Money, power, and material objects will not support you during bleak and lonely afternoons. Rich, generative relationships *will*, as will interests or activities that provide a wealth of emotional meaning. This is the time to find interests that give you a sense of becoming. The superficial aspects of your life will contribute to the grayness that you feel in your depths. The grayer that you feel, the more insecure you will feel about your facade, and the more anguish you will suffer about what you feel to be your imperfections. The more you are obsessed with what you feel to be wrong with you, the more that you will expect other people to see you the same way.

Essentially, what you tend to do is create a tight, rigid "reality" in your head that you then think of as the expectations of the world and about which you feel simultaneously cautious and defensive. Because you tend to get so locked within your own ego, it is difficult for you to see how your cold, defensive, or insecure behavior pushes people in the opposite direction. It is likely that you may be doing that a lot during this period and therefore may be in deep anguish over the disappointments that this behavior is eliciting.

The challenge now is to let yourself go emotionally, to enjoy yourself enough to get pleasure sharing the best aspects of your nature with the people you care about most. It is a time to try to stop worrying about how people see you and instead to try to obtain pleasure in the beauty and happiness you can bring someone else. If that happiness and love is not returned by one person, it will be by another—if you can stop worrying, fearing, and anguishing, and just begin to cultivate and enjoy all the beauty you already have inside of you. If you concentrate more on giving love to yourself and another person, or people, you will eventually receive the love that you need. Everyone loves a positive person who thoroughly enjoys himself or herself. Likewise, everyone responds to the negativity of a person who can only think in terms of criticism and rejection.

This is a time to turn yourself inside out and to begin with the inside. Make your life larger than life Concentrate on how many friends you have who love you, not on what you do not have. Begin a program of self-improvement that begins with making a list of all the ways you have improved as a human being in the last five years. When you look in the mirror, mentally make a count of all the things that you enjoy about your features. Never compare yourself to people who have more—beauty, youth, money, friends, lovers, luck. Instead, concentrate, every single day, on the unique qualities and attributes you have that no one else has. Never identify your ego with a diminishing situation. Instead, try to stand back from it, tell yourself it will pass, and try to learn something from the experience that will make you stronger, wiser, and richer as a human being. Try to realize the degree to which you color emotional situations by your negative expectations. Finally, instead of being hard on yourself and other people, concentrate on enjoying being kind to yourself and other people.

The Capricorn nature that has matured emotionally to the point of loving freely offers its own human beauty in response to the human beauty of another person, gaining every moment from the rich quality of the experience. The Capricorn who loves in bondage, defensively, risks feeling only in order to gain a part of himself, the self that he has yet to discover within. That is why security is sought so intensely and abandonment is feared so profoundly. Should a relationship end abruptly or explosively, as often happens under this transit when the individual is very young physically or emotionally, the emotional impact can be so devastating that it is deathlike, for the partner had become an unconscious projection of the ego. However, to the degree that the ego and inner depths are richly developed, there is a person, not a cavity, to fall back on, and new positive experiences will pop up along the way.

Under this transit, it is the potential of your nature to learn one all-or-nothing lesson, and that is that your suffering comes really from the rigidity of your fear.

Your life will improve profoundly now, to the degree

that you try to lighten it of all the negative emotional baggage you so compulsively impose. This is not easy by any means. It might very well be the hardest task that you have ever undertaken. But it is within you to grow deeper and wiser and happier as you grow older, generating all the love and life that you so long for. However much effort this takes—however many paths, trial-and-error love affairs—your effort will be rewarded because you will see the difference in the quality of your life.

During this period, you will many times reevaluate yourself and your life. If, despite setbacks and temporary circumstances, you are growing wiser and getting happier as you get older, you are doing something right. But if the only changes are in your bank account and the digits of your age, your heart is in serious trouble. Acknowledging this is the first step to changing the emptiness and growing beyond it to generate love, life, and ceaseless possibility.

Uranus Square the Sun in Aquarius

This is a cycle of subtle tensions and pressures that at times may build to a point of high-strung hysteria, nervousness, mental agitation, and tightly controlled but unexpressed anger. In extreme cases, the stress to the nervous system could be so great that it could result in an emotional breakdown. However, this is rare and more likely to happen with Aquarius on the ascendant.

The sun is in its detriment in the sign of Aquarius, which means that there is a poor sense of self and very often a low sense of self-esteem. Aquarius is a self-detached, other-oriented sign that is often out of touch with its deeper feelings. Its approach to life is more cerebral than emotional. Therefore, anger is not easily expressed or recognized because much of life tends to be intellectualized.

Anger is a problem now as Uranus transits in square to your sign. At times it is a subliminal undercurrent that is barely noticeable. At other times it will be experienced as insomnia, and tightly wired nervous tension about people problems. When the anger does surface, it will be through interpersonal frictions that can increase to such intensity that they instigate altercations, quarrels, and divorces.

As Uranus transits from your solar tenth house, career pressures are felt intensely. There could be painful fluctuations in this area now, as unforeseen disappointments can be temporarily blinding. At the same time, the stress felt behind the pressure to perform can also increase to the point that it feels as if it's squeezing out your life force.

For many Aquarians, this is tranquilizer time, as internal pressures build up and the events of your life begin to have a roller-coaster effect on your sense of well-being. In many important aspects of your life there is a lack of a continuity now. At the same time, there is a deeper conscious need for things to stay safely in place and for there to be something dependable to look forward to.

This is a difficult time for love because the people you will tend to meet may appear unreliable, undependable, erratic, or emotionally compromised. The resulting disappointments from the experience of such behavior can lead to tremendous bitterness if you are not careful. To protect yourself, it is important to look before you leap and to watch for signals early on. Precipitous marriages formed under this aspect often fail because initially the partner was looked upon in terms of ideals rather than hardcore realistic values.

The square aspect of Uranus challenges positive change from within. When those changes are not made, the change still comes but it appears to be enforced from without. The difficulty of this angular relationship is that its tension elicits profound psychological and emotional conflict. Although the conflict will ultimately manifest as a situation in the everyday world, it will begin as an emotional or psychological blind spot within your own psyche. One part of you wants something very badly, and another part of you says that you can not have it and trusts that it will not happen. Such deep-seated conflict causes profound emotional tension, and when Uranus comes along with its higher octave energies that directly stimulate the nervous system, your mind may become so stressed that it runs in circles, causing sleepless nights and even anxiety and depression.

This can be a difficult transit to experience because the nervous tension can also become physical. Contemplative solitude is helpful now, as is physical exercise. Within the solitude it is important to do everything from meditating to listening to relaxing music in order to soothe your mind and gain a greater perspective on your problems.

This is a very important time in which you should work to make constructive changes in your life. The first change you have to make is to decrease the negativity of your self-image. Greater self-acceptance and self-trust must be cultivated now, and it won't be easy. What you have inside of you is all that you ever really have to fall back upon. Therefore, it is essential to try to develop a center within yourself that grows stronger and stronger until eventually it is unshakable in the face of all externals.

One way to do this is to determine your unique individuality, what you have that is special and wonderful apart from everyone else, and develop that aspect of yourself on a committed basis. Secondly, you have to decide what you can change in yourself that would make you enjoy *you* more. Make a list of these changes and go over them on a daily basis. Begin with superficials, which might have to do with dieting, exercise, clothes. Then go into longstanding emotional and psychological areas that have to do with such things as specific fears, shyness, negative competitiveness (comparing yourself to people you think have more), negative feelings you have about your body or your personality or your looks. Try to do at least one major thing each week that makes you take greater pleasure in yourself and that instills change and growth as well.

This might be a time when you might want to

explore psychotherapy—go back into it, if you have left it, or explore other types of human potential groups. Group therapy could be especially helpful now because it would aid you in seeing parts of your self-diminishing behavior that you may have become blind to.

New positive attitudes must be developed now if you are going to grow and benefit from the growth. Also, new positive, affirmative, people should be cultivated along with more life-enhancing interpersonal experiences.

Stand back from your life, as you would from a game that you can walk away from at any minute. From this perspective, make it like a game, that is, your own personal and very special creation. Now, of course, interferences and disappointments will disrupt it. However, do not allow them to diminish you. Keep to the track and to the achievement of your goals. When you feel tempted to give in and feel sorry for yourself, just stop and think about how much more light you will bring to yourself if you accomplish at least a few of your goals.

This is an important weeding out period in your life. To make room for positive new feelings and experiences, it will be necessary to do some emotional accounting. This is the time to put your personal relationships on a benefit-cost ratio. If they are costing you more than they are giving you, then you should carefully consider releasing yourself from the experience. Relationships do not have to last forever, and some shouldn't. However, the important thing is that you have to start to see yourself as the one who decides that.

If you have invested yourself in a love experience that has hurt and disappointed you, try to see the situation in a larger perspective. Try to get beyond your bruised ego and burned expectations by asking yourself some of the following questions: Was that person, from the start, telling you through their behavior things about themselves that you would not allow yourself to see? Did you, out of feeling grateful for the affection and attention, settle for thoughtless, inconsiderate behavior that was not commensurate with your worth as a person? Did you encourage this behavior by failing to express your honest feelings or to set up definitive parameters that demonstrated to the other person your own sense of self-worth? Did you continually make excuses and rationalize their behavior when it was obvious that you were unhappy with the situation and not getting back what you felt you were giving?

It might be possible that from the start this person could not meet your emotional needs. If so, the next time you owe it to yourself to be clearer about the signals before you become involved. One of the reasons that you have a tendency to block is that you fear that you will never find such a stimulating situation again. However, the only thing that stands in your way is your own fear, which is constantly feeding you the wrong information. This is the time to acknowledge these fears openly and work through them slowly and patiently. It is also the time to begin to discover your richest sense of self, perhaps to manifest it in its highest image, and then to assert it in only the most positive ways.

Whatever falls through in your life now, you must not try to cling to. New, wonderful people and experiences await you if you just keep your heart open to the possibility. This will take tremendous courage, but you have that courage within you.

The doctrine at the core of Taoism is what is called the *Wu Wei* philosophy. What that means is training the mind to flow with change, not against it, so that you are not brutalized by it. You must behave as affirmatively as possible while trusting that the change has its own meaning to your psyche and that one day you will understand that unique meaning with a liberating wisdom that will propagate more positive situations.

Uranus is the planet of blinding change, the kind of change that easily puts the average mind out of control. The challenge now is to develop some of the attitude of the *Wu Wei* philosophy and generate a more dispassionate outlook on life that opens the heart and the mind to more affirmative, liberating perspectives. To view these perspectives, the mind has to begin to think in new ways from the center of an unshaken affirmative individuality. These new ways will ultimately bring the growth of a new, more affirmative person who is no longer enslaved by self-inflicted fears of limitation. The positive keyword now is freedom. You must work to rid yourself of all self-imposed limitations and experience the joy of feeling free in your center. Let this cycle, with all its frustrations, be a cycle that begins the unfolding of a new self. Then think of the day when you will look back upon your present self from a much happier place. While you do that, affirm every day that what you want will become you.

Saturn Square the Sun in Aquarius

The chief difficulty of this period is a leaden feeling that often diminishes the vital sense of self and life. Saturn is the taskmaster of the zodiac, and under Saturn transits, which come every seven years, come life lessons that offer the potential of self-mastery and growth. Saturn brings into the life of an individual a learning time. It is an opportunity to stop, pause, and reflect upon one's self and its relationship to the goings on in one's life. Under the influence of Saturn one tends to view one's life in the least pleasant way. Life appears flawed and the imperfections seem to impose themselves on the vital awareness. Usually, the meaningless, lackluster tediousness of the mundane world blankets the consciousness now, and ideally, a search is begun for richer values and more meaningful pastimes.

Saturn is the lord of karma. Karma means simply that what we think and what we do comes back on us to either make us suffer or bring us joy. Therefore, the greatest lesson to be learned under the transit of Saturn is the necessity of always trying to do the best by ourselves so that we can experience the greatest peace and joy. This may sound simple. However, often our motivations are confused in our own minds. Actions are born from fear, guilt, pent-up anger, or the irrational compulsion to be self-sacrificing to win approval.

What Saturn is testing now is the self and its power. Therefore, at times during this cycle, life may feel like a tightrope on which your mind is being stretched. Tension, fatigue, anxiety, depression, and sickness are some of the negative ways that the brain often chooses to cope with this transit. However, they aren't the only ways. Each unique conflict also has its own positive answer, and the challenge is to find it within one's deepest reaches. However, the greatest challenge of all is to make the search an adventure into the self.

Each problem that you encounter now is like a Zen koan. A Zen koan is a paradoxical question, such as "What is the sound of one hand clapping?" As ridiculous as this question may sound, there is an answer that can be achieved in an intuitive flash after meditating. Such, also, is the nature of our problems. During the onset and experience of a problem, life feels weighty and the entire sense of living is dimmed. Problems are like traps. They make us creaturely and animallike as they annihilate our lofty aspirations. However, if one learns how to meditate with oneself, to go into oneself and to ask questions, the answers will always come eventually and the light will return and grow.

The questions must go something like this: Why is this *really* happening? What is it in myself, what fear, what guilt, what irrational thought-form that is preventing me from being blissfully happy right now? What am I thinking to hold myself back? Come to the understanding that there is an answer to these questions, and when the answer comes, it will be a revelation that will bring you to a new level of self-awareness. Employing this self-awareness diligently and constructively, you can work to eventually bring about the changes that you want.

However, keep in mind that it will happen slowly. The more unhappy you are with yourself and your life, the more slowly the answers will come. But you must also believe that the answers *will* come. If you cannot believe that, or that you have the power within you to liberate yourself from your sorrow, you never will, and most likely the darkness will increase with age.

Under the transit of Saturn you must start to learn some of these lessons, or you will make yourself suffer deeply. However, if you treat all experiences as learning experiences and try to aim for total consciousness, you will always have something wonderful to look forward to because with each mental flash your heart will get lighter and your life brighter. When we are not learning our lessons under Saturn, which means feeling like a helpless victim in the face of disappointment, life starts to look like a tiny, dirty, room with all the shades drawn. However, when we have mastered our emotional-spiritual lessons, which means realizing emotionally and not merely intellectually that our minds are powerful instruments that create the conditions of our reality, we also realize that we can change our "reality" by changing our way of thinking. At this point, life begins to look more like a chandelier-lit room.

During this cycle, the experience of life will be like being in a Zen Buddhist temple. Such a place often inspires fear, misery, and dread in the hearts of the disciples because of the rigorous, diminishing disciplines that go on there, imposed by the master on his pupils when they fail to respond correctly to the questions of the Zen koans. This is directly analogous to life when we fail to answer our own questions. In Zen it is the common practice that when a pupil fails to respond correctly, or worse responds with arrogance, he is rapped painfully on the head or hand with a ruler. When he is hit enough times, after enough sessions with the master, eventually the answer comes. In life, when we make choices for ourselves that are self-diminishing, the conditions that ultimately arise, hit us over the head. It is painful, for certain. However, the crucial point that I want to make is that it is absolutely necessary that we do not allow these blows to define us, our worth, or our sense of possibility. See each blow, not as a condition, *but as a question*, and a question that you will one day be able to answer for your self and thereby be that much more enlightened.

The more we are enlightened, the lighter and brighter we feel. The more that we exist unconsciously and mechanically, the darker and heavier. The goal is to become master. The Zen master is master of his disciples only in that he is master of himself. As every limiting human impulse pops up in his consciousness, he knows its answer, and furthermore he knows how to make the answer work for him.

Because the sun is in its detriment in Aquarius, there is a poor sense of self and self-esteem that must be worked on. Because Aquarius is such an other-oriented sign, it often makes choices that work against the self and limits the sense of possibility. Underlying these choices is a conviction that one does not really deserve or that people who get rewards are the least deserving, which is a projection of a nondeserving self. The self-projection is often negative in this sign and demonstrates self-doubt and a conspicuous lack of self-love. This behavior is always picked up, sometimes consciously and always unconsciously, by the minds of others, who often treat the Aquarius person the way he or she projects they expect to be treated. However, that is not the way they *want* to be treated, and this frustrating conflict further diminishes their self-value until the cycle becomes a complicated, insidious process. At this point the second Aquarius personality problem comes to bear, and that is anger. Because there is a tendency initially not to set up affirmative parameters and behavioral expectations, situations can get so compromising that when the built up anger comes, it is out of proportion to the entire situation and consequently very self-destructive. Often the anger is not expressed at all but turned inward, where it seethes in a mire of depression.

During this Saturn cycle it is your opportunity to become aware of these tendencies in your personality and work them out so that they won't continue to limit you or your happiness. Because Saturn hits us every seven years, whatever is not learned now will come up again, and the conditions will be that much more difficult. It is crucial to keep in mind that the darkness catalyzed by a Saturn transit is the darkness of one's own individual consciousness. This is the time to probe it deeply to get to the light and to let that light define you. During this time try to turn each blackened experience into one of possibility that can ultimately work for you. As soon as you stop watching everybody else and simply allow yourself to deserve, you will be where you are supposed to be. Once you get on that sidewalk, you will never go back again. You will just keep growing, and growing brighter.

Pluto Square the Sun in Aquarius

This life cycle is a long, slow changing one in the depths of your being. Pluto brings about death and rebirth situations that can be painful because they force us to confront our essence, stripped of all defenses, props, and subterfuge. Our unconscious being seems to rise up and show itself in ways that are often frightening because the feelings seem to compromise the will and the needs of the ego. Mysterious moods arise, escalate, and fall away. Conditions and relationships end, often painfully. There is often confusion about who you really are and where you are going. Meaning becomes a keyword and you begin to question the meaning of your life and your emotional experiences.

Greater meaning is needed now, as a sense of meaninglessness can become pervasive. This is a time when you may feel emotionally beside yourself, painfully detached and disconnected from the sense of a much needed deeper power. And this feeling of disconnection can give birth to a feeling of loneliness in the soul.

Love is yearned for now as comfort and protection against the encroaching world. However, love experiences entered into desperately now require a painful price. This is primarily because the psyche is searching for the love in another person that it is not getting in itself.

The unbearable anguish often experienced during a Pluto transit to the sun sign has to do with a sense of blocked power. Therefore, there is often an increased drive for external power as a compensation. Sometimes there is also an ego clash with an authority figure, which can provoke a disturbing sense of inadequacy. This is a time when self-doubt and recrimination can rise up and distort your well-being, as you are beginning to doubt old conditions, situations, and relationships that have become a part of you.

A new part of yourself is trying to be born now. Any emotional pain that you are undergoing has to do with resistances in your personality to the needed growth. Defense mechanisms that have become secure subterfuges are holding you back. It is a time to confront them and move beyond them.

People often enter psychotherapy during a Pluto transit to the sun sign because the emotional effect is profoundly complicated psychologically. As the unconscious needs and compulsions leak into the conscious mind the rational ordering becomes nebulous and confused. If your sense of self becomes dimmed and your will clouded, then there is no inner bastion to sustain you emotionally. Successful psychotherapy will help you unravel your defense mechanisms and reveal your unique spark that has the potential of growing into a stronger, brighter sense of self.

Pluto is the planet of transformation, death, and rebirth. It often brings enforced change into the life through the unconscious compulsion for change. The changes instigated by Pluto, whether they are consciously created or unconsciously projected from the outside, have profound value for the quality of life. Sometimes the changes are apparently subtle, such as a change of feeling toward an old friend based on some momentary misunderstanding. However, what usually happens under Pluto is that this subtle change will be brooded over and grow in power. Ultimately it could lead, for example, to a complete reevaluation of the relationship, which may be no longer viable, but to a reevaluation of the quality of life and values. Therefore, what may have begun as a small incident, not terribly significant at the time, could ultimately result in a completely altered life-perspective, which may be positive or painful depending on the individual and how well they know and trust themselves.

In mythology Pluto was the ruler of the underworld. It is also the planet associated with the Mafia. There is a profoundly insidious quality to its vibrations and their effect upon conscious awareness. The marriages and love relationships that end under Pluto transits usually have been eroding in the consciousness for quite some time. There comes a point when the strain is unbearable, and in order to maintain the sense of self, a split has to come.

Frequently with Pluto squares, the love relationships take on a compulsive tone, and there is a strong tendency to renew the tie. Relationships formed when Pluto transits in square to the Sun are often complicated love-hate relationships that require some sacrifice of ego. Although these relationships are often painful they offer the potential of greater self-awareness if they are viewed from the perspective of a learning experience.

Depending on the individual's maturity, it will seem that many situations will require some self-sacrifice now. The challenge will be to say no to the sacrifice and yes to your own needs. Every conflict that comes into your life now must be seen as the motor of change. Likewise, all change must be treated as if it had a constructive purpose, leading you to a liberating lesson that will ultimately affirm yourself.

As I mention elsewhere, because the sun is in its detriment in Aquarius, this is a sign that must work to develop a strong, affirmative center for its own emotional well-being. Under the influence of the unconscious need for this greater wholeness impresses itself upon the quality of life.

Pluto has to do with emotional problems, and its painfully won wisdom is that we don't have to suffer our entire life because of them. However, we will suffer to the degree that we block our own unique potential. Pluto is the planet of elimination and renewal. It demands that we let go of the negative habits, compulsions, and relationships that are holding us back, to renew our attitudes, perspectives, and self-worth.

Because Pluto is the slowest-moving planet in the zodiac, being in a sign for several years, its effect upon the psyche is the deepest and its lessons the most difficult to learn for the mind that is unaware. For the more enlightened mind, eager to take its life into its own hands, this is a time when each emotional problem is looked upon as a valuable doorway to greater self-understanding and potential self-mastery. This is a time to become acquainted with the shadow, the darker, unacceptable inner reaches that often control the conscious personality through compulsion and obsession.

One practical way to do this is to keep a diary or daily log of your deepest thoughts, mental flashes, and dreams. This can be extremely valuable because as you begin to write, your pen will link the conscious with the unconscious and the thoughts and feelings that come through can help you see new dimensions of yourself. The wisdom deep inside you will also come through, and you may be surprised to see your own insights unraveling emotional conflicts. Wise sayings, aphorisms, and parables that you come across that have unique meaning in your life are also beneficial to put in the diary because this diary should ultimately become a treasured, elevating part of yourself.

If you see each emotional problem as a learning

experience that you record and reflect upon, in time you will be able to read over your life and see how your intelligence and wisdom has increased. Not only will you come away enjoying and respecting yourself more, but you will also be able to see the unfolding of your own consciousness as a fascinating process. Your problems will gain symbolic value as well and thereby lose a lot of their onerous emotional impact. When you learn to step outside yourself, the experience of living becomes more like an adventure that you're watching rather than a hopeless dead end supported by memories of past fears and failures.

Nothing is a failure if it can also be seen as an experience that will help you grow beyond yourself. In the long run, if viewed with enough wisdom and dispassion, the experience of what appeared to be a momentary ego "failure" may bring an awareness and inner experience that is many times more valuable.

Ultimately, the possible wisdom of Pluto helps us redefine the experience of winning and losing. Its tale is about the paradox of personal power, which is, essentially, that sometimes one has to be able to give something up in order to really have it. This holds true for relationships with others as well as with the self. It is a mysterious journey into self-trust and love that must be lived through in order to be realized. To get there is power. Every step along the way is a wondrous experience in itself that has the potential of growing into something more—something luminous, vital, and generative. You are moving toward a new you now. Keep that in mind as you seek to find the light behind every conflict and disappointment, and eventually your mind and heart will become that light. Then one day you will look back upon your darkness and smile.

Neptune Square the Sun in Pisces

The problems that arise during this cycle have to do with the use and abuse of your emotions. Neptune is the ruler of Pisces. Sitting in a mutable fire sign and squaring your sign, it will tend to make you more restless, idealistic, impressionable, and at times discontent. There will be a tendency to see your life more idiosyncratically now. Neptune is the planet associated with illusion. Because of the illusions we embrace we often suffer painful disillusionment. And during this cycle the pain that is felt is a result of the illusions that have been embraced about the life, the identity, or the relationships.

The challenge now is to sort out the inspirational from the illusory. The influence of Neptune makes one want to glamorize experience into self-created fantasy. The disappointments that arise now arise because of these attitudes.

The demands of the outside world may cause a tremendous compromise of your spirit now. Your ideals may demand one way for life to unfold, while reality may disappoint your expectations.

It is difficult to view either yourself or your life with objectivity now. Your self-image is not clear, and caught within that confusion are your compromised ideals. However, what you do not yet understand is that all disappointments now are due to your own lack of certainty about who you really are. You don't completely trust yourself, and that distrust is coming to the surface through problems, conflicts, or clashes with the external world.

It may seem that your sense of self, along with certain conditions in your life, is dissolving now, and you feel uncertain about who you really are, where you are going, and how you will be able to control your life in a way that is most affirmative.

It is likely that conditions will be rising to the surface now that you have refused to confront before. This is a time when you will pay a price for the things that you deliberately refuse to see. An inexplicable moodiness is often experienced during this time. At moments it may seem like you are caught in a dead end without any inspiration or any hope of a new beginning or an ideal beginning.

Anyone who is feeling bad under this transit is really suffering from a lack of psychological fluidity and a strong degree of cynicism. Pisces is a sign that holds in feeling and lets fear and rage become so rancid that they can erode the vitality of life. Therefore, if you are seriously apathetic, moody, or depressed now, it is partly because of your negative use of emotion and partly because you are looking at your life and yourself in a distorted fashion. There is a damaging undercutting trend in your personality, a tendency to diminish other people because you fear diminishment. This is a time to look at that squarely in the face and consider what it is all about. If you really loved yourself and trusted your ability to create and fulfill possibility, there would not be such a tendency to focus on the negativities of other people. A self-affirmed person concentrates on multiplying his or her own possibilities regardless of what may appear to be obstacles or disappointments at the time.

If you can't do this, it is because you can't love or trust yourself and probably make wrong decisions for yourself that make you feel angry and victimized. However, the truth is that when you are discontent, you are your favorite victim. The unsuccessful choices that you make are due to the narrowness of your own vision, your lack of self-trust, and your absence of a sense of self-worth.

When your anger and cynicism come to control you, your inner core turns into a blackened sun, and from that center it appears that there is no life-enhancing possibility anywhere around you. However this is a self-created illusion, sparked by negative thinking. This is a time when you must begin to change your attitudes about yourself. If you are unhappy, psychotherapy is essential now, because you must start to develop a strong inner center that will sustain you. However, that is merely a starting point. You must also think about what would give you a greater sense of peace, serenity, and emotional possibility, even if your life props were taken away from you.

If your heart is in a self-affirmed place, this life cycle could be one in which you follow your fantasies without fear and explore new aspects of yourself through new forms of creativity. It would be emotionally cathartic now to keep a journal of your feelings. If you are depressed, painting in a very thick tempera can give you the sense that you are pulling your feelings out and turning them into colors that are external to you. Make this a time when you take it upon yourself to create all sorts of new beginnings that revitalize your emotions and your experience of life.

This cycle has the potential of being an inspirational time when you get to know new aspects of yourself that you thoroughly enjoy. However, it is a time when you are more susceptible to romantic disappointment, because you are not seeing yourself or those close to you clearly. The more love and respect that you feel for yourself, the more you will be capable of attracting and experiencing a mature love. Try to see how you can grow from your emotional experiences now so that you feel more enlarged in your capacity for loving. If it is romantic disappointment from which you are suffering, make a list of all the characteristics you would like to find in a person. Read the list over to yourself at least twice daily as you visualize the person in your mind. If you do this long enough, you will attract this person to you. Test your own power and try it. What you may find is that you really can be master of your life.

Uranus Square the Sun in Pisces

Because yours is a mind that is ready and willing to see the world in new, unconventional ways, this could be an interesting life cycle, characterized by all kinds of change and a sharper intuitive awareness.

Uranus's effect on your nervous system will be to enhance your perceptive powers now. You will find that you are beginning to see life in new ways and that you have a need to experience novel things as well.

As you pass through this life cycle you will increasingly feel a need for change. The deepest part of you seeks a greater freedom of self-expression and possibility. It is a time of explorations, the birth of new hopes, unexpected endings, and new beginnings. New sensations, needs, and inspirations will be awakened in you. And it is the period in which to push yourself to take risks and rise to their call.

Anything that holds you back or circumscribes your sense of freedom will be resented more intensely now. This is a time when your entire being rebels against being confined by the absurdity of meaningless limitations. For the past couple of years you have been insistently feeling emotional frustrations in your life. Whether it has been love, work, or problems with people close to you, you have felt pushed out of control by the pressure from the imposed limitations. Now you want to break free of limiting restrictions, even if you can't express these feelings overtly.

There will be a strong undercurrent of irritability

now when things don't happen as you would like them to ideally. At times your temper may get the better of you, and you may take it out on anyone who happens to be close. Try to be constructive in your approach to the changes you most want to make because, in the long run, you are the one who suffers most from your emotions. The difficulty during this period is that people around you will prove erratic, unreliable, and often downright provocative. The result will be that you will feel angry and have little faith in many words of trust. At other times, through disruptive change, you may feel as if the floor has been pulled out from underneath you. However, although some things will fall through, other opportunities will also spring to life unexpectedly. Therefore, it is important not to allow yourself to become cynical about the bad times.

Your brain and entire nervous system will be highly stimulated now. This is an excellent time to receive intuitive flashes, to see your life in liberating ways, and to experiment with changes that will free you psychologically and spiritually.

This is also a time when you might want to make major career changes that you have been considering for some time. However, there will be a tendency to be precipitous now, and because of that, you will have to take special care to think of all future considerations and not merely of the moment. Frictions with a boss or a significant work colleague may incite you to do something that you may be sorry for later on. Therefore, be sure that the changes you bring about are ones that are the most affirmative for your particular life situation.

It is important to respond rather than react to all the influences around you now. If you feel conflicted by a nagging problem that has a rebarbative effect upon your brain, try to silence the external and internal voices and go inside the deepest part of yourself to find the answers that are already a part of you. Relationships often break up precipitously under this aspect because one looks at the other person, or one's life with him or her, in a new way. Sometimes there is a blinding need for freedom that emerges, and the person feels that he or she must follow it at all cost.

Long-term conflicts are seen as limitations to the sense of freedom now, and often there is an overwhelming desire to cut loose. At the worst moments you may feel emotionally unstable and blindly driven to exert your will. Frantic, irrational behavior could have a profoundly destructive effect on your entire well-being. Therefore, try to communicate your needs and expectations more directly so that the other party will understand your position. A primary Piscean problem is that feelings are not readily verbalized. The result is that communication problems arise, and consequently there is unnecessary conflict and confusion. The more blindly you behave right now, the more you will bring suffering upon yourself.

Often during this cycle there is a need for excitement and novelty that bears little consideration for human feeling. You may now want to try new things that are disruptive or destructive to the flow of your life or relationship. The important thing to keep in mind is that you must ultimately bear the responsibility for the moves that you make. Karma is responsibility. It means that what we do comes back on us either through reinforcement or sacrifice. If we make the wrong moves out of unbalanced emotions, we will ultimately have to deal with the consequences and the consequences can be extremely painful.

It happens to be a negative Piscean characteristic to feel uniquely victimized by situations that are disappointing or extremely limiting. Often the first impulse is to compare oneself to others who appear undeservedly happy and then to feel angry and bitter because it seems that you try harder and have less. This is a time to realize the profound destructiveness of this tendency. Not only is it cruelly self-diminishing, it is also counterproductive to seeing your own life as possibility.

Whatever falls through now, try not to identify your ego with it. See it as change that you can learn from, and then identify your ego with the positive aspects of your life that reflect your unique intelligence and sensitivity. Try to see the imposed changes in your life as portals to potential opportunity. When something ends painfully, allow yourself the time to heal. Then sit back from the experience as if it were someone else's life. From this perspective try to glean how your faulty thinking obfuscated your perceptions of the whole situation. Then contemplate how you can make changes in your thinking and behavior so that it doesn't happen again.

Finally, try to see that the most important change that you must make in your life now is in terms of your own self-love. Regardless of what is happening on the outside, look at your life only in terms of greater possibility. Make this a daily mental discipline, and in a matter of months your life will change.

Cycles of the Slow-Moving Planets

Sun Sign	Phenomena	Dates	Page
Aries	Saturn Opposition Sun	9/1980–11/1982 5/1983–8/1983	65
	Pluto Opposition Sun	8/1972–11/1983 5/1984–9/1984	69
Taurus	Saturn Opposition Sun	12/1982–5/1983 9/1983–11/1985	73
	Uranus Opposition Sun	9/1975–11/1981	78
	Pluto Opposition Sun	11/1983–5/1984 9/1984–11/1995	81
Gemini	Uranus Opposition Sun	11/1981–2/1988	87
	Neptune Opposition Sun	11/1970–11/1984	90
Cancer	Saturn Square Sun	9/1980–11/1982 5/1983–8/1983	94
	Pluto Square Sun	8/1972–4/1983 5/1984–9/1984	100
Leo	Saturn Square Sun	12/1982–5/1983 9/1983–11/1985	103
	Uranus Square Sun	9/1975–11/1981	107
	Pluto Square Sun	11/1983–5/1984 9/1984–11/1995	110

Sun Sign	Phenomena	Dates	Page
Virgo	Uranus Square Sun	11/1981–2/1988	115
	Neptune Square Sun	11/1970–11/1984	120
Libra	Saturn Conjunct Sun	9/1980–11/1982 5/1983–8/1983	125
	Pluto Conjunct Sun	8/1972–11/1983 5/1984–9/1984	129
Scorpio	Saturn Conjunct Sun	12/1982–5/1983 9/1983–11/1985	133
	Uranus Conjunct Sun	9/1975–11/1981	141
	Pluto Conjunct Sun	11/1983–5/1984 9/1984–11/1995	145
Sagittarius	Neptune Conjunct Sun	11/1970–11/1984	148
	Uranus Conjunct Sun	11/1981–2/1988	152
Capricorn	Saturn Square Sun	9/1980–11/1982 5/1983–8/1983	155
	Pluto Square Sun	8/1972–11/1983 5/1984–9/1984	159
Aquarius	Uranus Square Sun	9/1975–11/1981	166
	Saturn Square Sun	12/1982–5/1983 9/1983–11/1985	172
	Pluto Square Sun	11/1983–5/1984 9/1984–11/1995	177
Pisces	Neptune Square Sun	11/1970–11/1984	182
	Uranus Square Sun	11/1981–2/1988	186

Conclusion

Transformation is inextricable from growth. This book has been about the entire process of growth leading to transformation, beginning with the pain of astrologically induced personal and psychological crisis. Potentially, we can all grow, emotionally and psychologically, through committed psychotherapy in which we work to unfold the unconscious part of our personality and blend it into our consciousness to become more whole. However, this type of change usually is not quite as dramatic or as rapid as the change the personality undergoes when it has to cope with crisis.

Although we would all enjoy a life of constant pleasure, we would not grow wiser, stronger, or more intelligent from such a life. The greater the amount of wisdom that a human being has within to call upon, the greater is his or her serenity during the bad times. Essentially the nature of human existence is that one suffers until one has attained enough wisdom to be able to apply it in life.

The practical purpose of astrology is that it gives us a deeper understanding of our inner dynamics; it can also give insights into the planets as electromagnetic force-fields exerting influences on our individual psyches. The practical purpose of a mystical perspective is that it leads to a slow, steady accrual of wisdom that will make the experience of living much easier. Your job may still fall through, your partner may leave, and your friends may disappoint you, and, of course, you will feel the pain. However, you do not hold on to it and it does not define you. You learn to relax deep inside of yourself and let it pass away along with the person or experience, *all the while trusting* that in the future, something more meaningful will come along.

What mysticism does essentially is give a person a way of looking at their life on a moment-to-moment basis that is ultimately affirmative. It is a new, positive way of seeing life and oneself that is self-liberating. But it is a way of thinking that must be learned and diligently practiced to be effective. Also, before this mode of thinking can be effective, a very strong, affirmative center has to be developed, one that evolves through the capacity of self-love into a higher self. An experience of the higher self is one of those rare moments in life when you have loved yourself, those close to you, and your life with a deep inner bliss. When the higher consciousness develops, this experience becomes more and more frequent, until in the highest states it floods the entire being. With a disciplined, well-trained mind, it is possible to bring about this serenity even in times of crisis, so that the experience of severance is not experienced as one of loss.

This is almost impossible for the average human mind to conceive of, yet every human being who is not retarded is capable of it. However, it is the nature of humanity to cling to the status quo, to fear change, and to feel victimized by their own painful circumstances. Crisis breaks up the status quo and makes change inevitable. The astrological cycles of the slow moving planets instigate all sorts of crises in the minds and lives of individuals who have not had their higher faculties awakened. In doing so, they make room for greater possibility. The first step toward that possibility is to ask yourself questions: Do I really need this terrible marriage, why am I doing this to myself, why am I assigning all this power to a person who doesn't matter as much as I do, what am I really trying to escape from by being sick, what is it that I can't face here, why am I still in a relationship with someone who really isn't nice to me? The second step is to find some answers and make changes that are better for you, that affirm your sense of being, that enlarge your perspective on your own life. The third step is to work, every single day, on developing a greater degree of self-love. For the terrible pain that comes with a life crisis arises because the self is not affirmed enough to trust itself to create positive new beginnings out of the chaos. However, with the right attitude, the death of every circumstance is accompanied by incipient rebirth.

I once met a very vital woman, a fashion designer who had so many interests and projects that her chief frustration was her lack of time. In getting to know her better I learned that two years before she had been on her deathbed in the last stages of cancer—her hair had completely fallen out and her expected time on earth was very short. This woman was the rebellious daughter of a Brahmin priest in India, and when she originally came to New York, it was her intention to make a lot of money, no matter how she did it. She had virtually no interest in her father's teachings and had cut herself completely free of her family.

Having extraordinary psychic powers, her father knew that she was close to death and contacted her. Essentially, he bid her farewell and tried his best to ease her passage into the next world. It was at that moment that she finally understood her own death, and in doing so began to also understand her own life. A miracle happened and she recovered completely. When I met this buoyantly healthy person, she had no physical concern except dieting. She would not tell me exactly what she did to create such a miraculous recovery.

However, she did say that with all of her will she changed her mind, her outlook, and her entire way of living. A third person, a fashion editor, was present who had visited her on her deathbed and attested to the horror of her entire being only two years before.

This woman is a most dramatic example of the kind of transformation that can take place through crisis. Coincidentally, I also know of another person who received this same astrological aspect. However, he did not have such a highly developed will or courage, and therefore the outcome for him was not so fortunate.

Many years ago, when I was a student of astrology, and very impressionable, I went to an astrologer to have my chart read. The astrologer told me outright that 1977 would be the next-to-the-worst year of my life, and that 1984 would definitely be the worst. For many years I lived with this terrible anxiety, which is one of the reasons why I personally frown upon the practices of so many people who call themselves psychics and astrologers.

It turned out that indeed 1977 was quite a gruesome year, characterized by my own dim level of consciousness. However, because I refuse to see any experience as anything but a learning experience, the emotional and psychological growth that I gained from that year was so absolutely extraordinary that it brought me to the threshold of a complete change in consciousness. A higher consciousness began to emerge very slowly, like a very dim light, until three years later another crisis triggered great illumination. Since then, in my life there have been a number of serious disappointments that have been like momentary pinpricks and were followed by many wonderful moments. Everyday I feel a sense of joy and peace that years ago was unimaginable. When I do experience pain now, I know it is because my attitude is wrong, and I call upon my inner wisdom to see the situation with greater clarity and dispassion. I no longer fear as I used to fear, and I certainly don't fear 1984, because my head has changed and I know how to utilize the power deep inside of me.

It all begins with growth. One must grow emotionally, intellectually, spiritually. One must educate one's mind, one must try to move beyond one's problems and limitations, one must try to know oneself, and, hardest of all, one must try to love oneself. Study and mental discipline are absolutely necessary for mystical or higher spiritual awareness. However, I have seen people study seriously for years, and watched the books in their library multiply, but their life never changes. The reason for this is that they don't know themselves, they have not pushed themselves to learn and grow from personal crises and disturbing experiences. Consequently, they have never learned the higher power of love.

The more you do affirmative things for yourself, despite crises and obstacles, the more you will be operating from the higher faculties of your being and the higher will be your experience of life and love. Teachings can be gotten from books, but they will remain mere intellectual concepts unless you work to get beyond your fear and rage and anxieties and get to that center of yourself that is pure LOVE. Once you get through all the layers of garbage, and it may take many years, and you finally hit upon the LOVE that is the highest aspect of your nature, your life will never be the same again, and from this high quality of experience you will never be able to go backward.

Such a joyous experience requires that growth be a goal. This book has been about astrologically induced cycles of growth and where they can potentially take you. In little ways I have tried to show you attitudes and practical techniques that you can develop that produce greater growth. More important, I have tried to show you that, for your own well-being, growth should be a *value*, and when it is a serious value, each stage of it will bring you to ever greater liberation.

Most people come to astrologers when they are in pain because they want to know when it will all be over. My point is that people should not even think in these terms. Acknowledge the pain but do not wait it out or roll around in it. Get behind it, let it take you somewhere. Ask yourself what it really means and how you can learn and grow from it. Finally, do not assign power to the pain. Stand back from it and assign power to yourself. People tend to treat their emotional pain as if it were a supreme authority that dictates their entire sense of possibility. Think of it only as a moment that has nothing to do with the future. Then sit down and dictate the future to yourself, despite the gloominess of Saturn and the hysteria of Uranus and the melancholy of Neptune and the depression of Pluto.

No matter what happens to you in life, after the first stunning blow, calculate and manipulate ways you can grow by it. Think only of *growth*. Paste it on your mirror. Paste it on your refrigerator. Put it on your pillow and think about it while in line at the bank. After a while your life will change. You will see it yourself, just as you will see yourself differently, and the reason for this will be that you have been transformed.

SUGGESTED BIBLIOGRAPHY

Suggested Bibliography

Arroyo, Stephen, *Astrology, Karma and Transformation.*
Assagioli, Roberto, *The Act of Will.*
———, *Psychosynthesis*
Baynes, C. F. and Richard Wilhelm, trans., *I Ching or Book of Changes.*
Becker, Ernest, *The Denial of Death.*
Blofeld, John, *The Secret and the Sublime.*
———, *Tantric Mysticism in Tibet.*
Bucke, Richard M., *Cosmic Consciousness.*
Capra, Fritjof, *The Tao of Physics.*
Cooper, J. C., *Taoism.*
Fromm, Eric, *The Art of Loving.*
Gallwey, Timothy, *The Inner Game of Tennis.*
Govinda, Lama, *The Way of the White Clouds.*
Greene, Liz, *Saturn.*
Herrigel, Eugen, *Zen in the Art of Archery.*
James, William, *Varieties of Religious Experience.*
Jung, Carl, *Pshychology and Alchemy.*
———, *Psychology and Religion: East and West.*
———, *Psychological Reflections*
Kaufmann, Walter, ed., *The Portable Nietzsche.*
Kierkegaard, Soren, *Fear and Trembling.*
———, *The Sickness unto Death.*
Kopp, Sheldon, *If You Meet the Buddha on the Road, Kill Him!*
Lao Tsu, *Tao Te Ching.*
Mann, Edward W., *Orgone, Reich and Eros.*
May, Rollo, *Love and Will.*
Nietzsche, Friedrich, *Beyond Good and Evil.*
———, *Ecce Homo.*
———, *The Will to Power.*
Ouspensky, P. D., *A New Model of the Universe.*
Pagels, Elaine, *The Gnostic Gospels.*
Reifler, Sam, *I Ching.*

Rilke, Rainer Maria, *Duino Elegies.*
————, *Poems from the Book of Hours.*
Roberts, Jane, *The Nature of Personal Reality. Seth Speaks.*
Rudhyar, Dane, *Galactic Dimension of Astrology,* (orig. title:)
    The Sun Is Also a Star.
Ruperti, Alexander, *Cycles of Becoming.*
Spinoza, Baruch, *The Ethics of Spinoza.*
Talbot, Michael, *Mysticism and the New Physics.*
Three Initiates, *The Kybalion.*
Tillich, Paul, *The Courage to Be.*
Von Eckartshausen, Karl, *The Cloud upon the Sanctuary.*
Watts, Alan, *Nature, Man and Woman.*
————, *This Is It.*
Wilhelm, Richard and Jung, C. G., *The Secret of the Golden
    Flower.*
Wood, Ernest, *Yoga.*
Yogananda, Paramahansa, *Autobiography of a Yogi.*

ABOUT THE AUTHOR

ROBIN MACNAUGHTON is the author of *Robin MacNaughton's Sun Sign Personality Guide*, *Robin MacNaughton's Moon Sign Personality Guide*, *How to Seduce Any Man in the Zodiac*, and a twelve-book guide to the complete personality of each astrological sign. She is presently living in New York City.

PSYCHIC WORLD

Here are some of the leading books that delve into the world of the occult—that shed light on the powers of prophecy, of reincarnation and of foretelling the future.

DON'T MISS
THESE CURRENT
Bantam Bestsellers

We Deliver!
And So Do These Bestsellers.

☐	23188	**BEVERLY HILLS DIET LIFETIME PLAN** by Judy Mazel	$3.95
☐	22661	**UP THE FAMILY TREE** by Teresa Bloomingdale	$2.95
☐	22701	**I SHOULD HAVE SEEN IT COMING WHEN** **THE RABBIT DIED** by Teresa Bloomingdale	$2.75
☐	22576	**PATHFINDERS** by Gail Sheehy	$4.50
☐	22585	**THE MINDS OF BILLY MILLIGAN** by Daniel Keyes	$3.95
☐	22981	**SIX WEEKS** by Fred Mustard	$2.95
☐	01428	**ALWAYS A WOMAN** (A Large Format Book)	$9.95
☐	22746	**RED DRAGON** by Thomas Harris	$3.95
☐	20687	**BLACK SUNDAY** by Thomas Harris	$3.50
☐	22685	**THE COSMO REPORT** by Linda Wolfe	$3.95
☐	22736	**A MANY SPLENDORED THING** by Han Suyin	$3.95
☐	20922	**SHADOW OF CAIN** by V. Bugliosi & K. Hurwitz	$3.95
☐	20230	**THE LAST MAFIOSO: The Treacherous** World of Jimmy Fratianno	$3.95
☐	13101	**THE BOOK OF LISTS #2** by I. Wallace, D. Wallechinsky, A. & S. Wallace	$3.50
☐	22771	**THE GREATEST SUCCESS IN THE WORLD** by Og Mandino	$2.75
☐	23271	**WHY DO I THINK I'M NOTHING WITHOUT** **A MAN?** by Dr. P. Russianoff	$3.50
☐	23296	**BH&G STEP-BY-STEP HOUSEHOLD REPAIRS** by BH&G Editors	$3.50
☐	20621	**THE PILL BOOK** by Dr. Gilbert Simon & Dr. Harold Silverman	$3.95
☐	23111	**GUINNESS BOOK OF WORLD RECORDS—** **21st ed.** by McWhirter	$3.95
☐	20303	**YOU CAN NEGOTIATE ANYTHING** by Herb Cohen	$3.50
☐	23084	**THE UMPIRE STRIKES BACK** by Ron Luciano	$3.50

Buy them at your local bookstore or use this handy coupon for ordering:

Bantam Books, Inc., Dept. NFB, 414 East Golf Road, Des Plaines, Ill. 60016

Please send me the books I have checked above. I am enclosing $_____
(please add $1.25 to cover postage and handling). Send check or money order
—no cash or C.O.D.'s please.

Mr/Mrs/Miss _____

Address_____

City_____ State/Zip_____

NFB—5/83

Please allow four to six weeks for delivery. This offer expires 11/83.
